MW01129480

The
BEST
of
HUMANISM

The BEST of HUMANISM

edited by Roger E. Greeley

Published in Cooperation with the North American Committee for Humanism

PROMETHEUS BOOKS
Buffalo, New York

THE BEST OF HUMANISM. Copyright © 1988 by Roger E. Greeley. All rights reserved. Printed in the United States of America. No part of this book may be used or reproduced in any manner whatsoever without written permission, except in the case of brief quotations embodied in critical articles and reviews. Inquiries should be addressed to Prometheus Books, 700 East Amherst Street, Buffalo, New York 14215.

91 90 89 88   4 3 2 1

Library of Congress Card Catalog No. 87-43317
ISBN: 0-87975-381-1

Contents

Acknowledgment

The editor wishes to express his deepest thanks to two people who assisted in the preparation of this anthology.

First, I must recognize Sherwin T. Wine for the support, enthusiasm, good counsel, and labors on behalf of this volume. We spent many hours culling through hundreds of selections we accumulated during the life of this project. As president of the North American Committee for Humanism, Sherwin's initial impetus and recommendations are largely responsible for my having done this work.

Second, I thank Dr. Hardy Carroll of Western Michigan University, who painstakingly tracked down the authorship and publication data of many of the contributions included in this anthology. His professional expertise made our job much easier.

The
BEST
of
HUMANISM

PART I

All About "God"

All About "God"

Central to every traditional and orthodox religion is some concept of "God" or "gods." Humanists consider the question of God irrelevant to their philosophy of living and the values upon which their ethics rest. Humanists nevertheless live in a world in which hundreds of millions embrace and rely on some kind of God concept. It does not serve Humanists well simply to dismiss any and all concepts of God without being able to discuss intelligently such concepts as deism, theism, atheism, agnosticism, polytheism, process theology, and other concepts with which individuals identify. The overwhelming majority of Humanists came to Humanism after rejecting some form of the Judeo-Christian tradition. Often, in looking back, Humanists are very negative in describing what remains for some an ennobling and hopeful concept. Should not Humanists be recognized by what they can affirm, by their conduct of life, and by their contribution to enlightenment here and now, rather than by the quality of their debunking?

While debunking is part of the catharsis every "come-outer" experiences, too often Humanists have stalled out in their negative rebellion against the religion or church of their formative years. The challenge to Humanists is to be able to communicate effectively the values that stand in place of a God concept but which serve as an affirmative governor in their conduct of life. Unless we are able to reveal through our behavior and our rhetoric compelling evidence

19

for the worth of Humanism, we shall fail as a movement. Where Humanists stand today requires an examination of how we got where we are. This section considers the question of God, and life lived without a notion of God, as viewed by many notable Humanists.

Agnosticism

Clarence Darrow

I do not consider it an insult, but rather a compliment to be called an agnostic. I do not pretend to know, where many ignorant men are sure—that is all agnosticism means.

Thomas Henry Huxley

I was brought up in the strictest school of evangelical orthodoxy; and when I was old enough to think for myself I started upon my journey of inquiry with little doubt about the general truth of what I had been taught; and with that feeling of the unpleasantness of being called an "infidel" which, we are told, is so right and proper. Near my journey's end, I find myself in a condition of something more than mere doubt about these matters.

In the course of other inquiries, I have had to do with fossil remains which looked quite plain at a distance, and became more and more indistinct as I tried to define their outline by close inspection. There was something there—something which, if I could win assurance about it, might mark a new epoch in the history of the earth; but, study as long as I might, certainty eluded my grasp. So has it been with me in my efforts to define the grand figure of Jesus as it lies in the primary strata of Christian literature. Is he the kindly, peaceful Christ depicted in the Catacombs? Or is he the stern Judge who frowns above the altar of SS. Cosmas and Damianus? Or can he be rightly represented by the bleeding ascetic, broken down by physical pain, of too many medieval pictures? Are we to accept the Jesus of the second, or the Jesus of the fourth Gospel, as the true Jesus? What did he really say and do; and how much that is attributed to him, in speech and action, is the embroidery of the various parties into which his followers tended to split themselves within twenty years of his death, when even the threefold tradition was only nascent?

If anyone will answer these questions for me with something more to the point than feeble talk about the "cowardice of Agnosticism," I shall be deeply his debtor. Unless and until they are satisfactorily answered, I say of Agnosticism in this matter, *"J'y suis, et j'y reste. . . ."*

When I reached intellectual maturity, and began to ask myself whether I was an atheist, a theist, or a pantheist, a materialist or an idealist, a Christian or a freethinker, I found that the more I learned and reflected, the less ready was the answer. . . . The one thing upon which most of these good people were agreed was the one thing in which I differed from them. They were quite sure they had attained a certain "gnosis"—had more or less successfully solved the problem of existence; while I was quite sure that I had not, and had a pretty strong conviction that the problem was insoluble. . . . This was my situation when I had the good fortune to find a place among the members of that remarkable confraternity of antagonists, . . . the Metaphysical Society. Every variety of philosophical and theological opinion was represented there; . . . most of my colleagues were -*ists* of one sort or another; and . . . I, the man without a rag of belief to cover himself with, could not fail to have some of the uneasy feelings which must have beset the historical fox when, after leaving the trap in which his tail remained, he represented himself to his normally elongated companions. So I took thought, and invented what I conceived to be the appropriate title of "agnostic." It came into my head as suggestively antithetic to the "gnostic" of Church history, who professed to know so much about the very things of which I was ignorant. . . . To my great satisfaction the term took. . . .

I am very well aware, as I suppose most thoughtful people are in these times, that the process of breaking away from old beliefs is extremely unpleasant; and I am much disposed to think that the encouragement, the consolation, and the peace afforded to earnest believers in even the worst forms of Christianity are of great practical advantage to them. What deductions must be made from this gain on the score of the harm done to the citizen by the ascetic other-worldliness of logical Christianity; to the ruler, by the hatred, malice, and all uncharitableness of sectarian bigotry; to the legislator, by the spirit of exclusiveness and domination of those that count themselves pillars of orthodoxy; to the philosopher, by the restraints on the freedom of learning and teaching which every Church exercises, when it is strong enough; to the conscientious soul, by the introspective hunting after sins of the mint and cummin type, the fear of theological error, and the overpowering terror of possible damnation, which have accompanied the Churches like their shadow, I need not now consider; but they are assuredly not small. If Agnostics lose heavily on the one side, they gain a good deal on the other. People who talk about the comforts of belief appear to forget its discomforts; they ignore the fact that the Christianity of the Churches is something more than faith in the ideal personality of Jesus, which they create for themselves, *plus* so much as can be carried into practice—without disorganizing civil society—of the maxims of the Sermon on the Mount. Trip in morals or in doctrine (especially in doctrine), without due repentance or retraction, or fail to get properly baptized before you die, and a *plebiscite* of the Christians of Europe, if they were true to their creeds, would affirm your everlasting damnation by an immense majority.

*   *   *

Agnosticism is not properly described as a "negative" creed, nor indeed as a creed of any kind, except in so far as it expresses absolute faith in the validity of a principle, which is as much ethical as intellectual. This principle may be stated in various ways, but they all amount to this: that it is wrong for a man to say that he is certain of the objective truth of any proposition unless he can produce evidence which logically justifies that certainty. This is what Agnosticism asserts; and in my opinion, it is all that is essential to Agnosticism. That which Agnostics deny, and repudiate as immoral, is the contrary doctrine, that there are propositions which men ought to believe, without logically satisfactory evidence; and that reprobation ought to attach to the profession of disbelief in such inadequately supported propositions. The justification of the Agnostic principle lies in the success which follows upon its application, whether in the field of natural, or in that of civil, history; and in the fact that, so far as these topics are concerned, no sane man thinks of denying its validity.

Atheism

Clarence Darrow

I don't believe in God because I don't believe in Mother Goose.

Eric Hoffer

The opposite of the religious fanatic is not the fanatical atheist but the gentle cynic who cares not whether there is a god or not. The atheist is a religious person. He believes in atheism as though it were a new religion. . . . So too, the opposite of the chauvinist is not the traitor but the reasonable citizen who is in love with the present and has no taste for martyrdom and the heroic gesture.

Bertrand Russell

At the age of eighteen, shortly before I went to Cambridge, I read Mill's *Autobiography,* where I found a sentence to the effect that his father taught him that the question "Who made me?" cannot be answered, since it immediately suggests the further question "Who made God?" This led me to abandon the "First Cause" argument, and to become an atheist. Throughout the long period of religious doubt I had been rendered very unhappy by the gradual loss of belief, but when the process was completed, I found to my surprise that I was quite glad to be done with the whole subject.

God

Paul Henri Thiry d'Holbach

Theology is but the ignorance of natural causes reduced to a system.
. . . [It] is a science that has for its object only things incomprehensible.
Contrary to all other sciences, it treats only of what cannot fall under
our senses. Hobbes calls it *the kingdom of darkness.* It is a country
in which everything is governed by laws contrary to those which
men can recognize in the world they inhabit. In this marvellous region,
light is no more than darkness; evidence is doubtful or false;
impossibilities are credible; reason is a deceitful guide; and good sense
becomes madness. This science is called theology, and this theology
is a continual insult to the reason of man. . . .

Does it require anything but plain common sense to perceive that
a being incompatible with the obvious facts of experience, that a cause
continually opposed to the effects which we attribute to it, that a being
of whom we can say nothing without falling into contradiction, that
a being who, far from explaining the mysteries of the universe, only
makes them more inexplicable: that a being to whom for so many
centuries men have so vainly addressed themselves to obtain their
happiness and the end of their suffering—does it, I say, require anything
more than plain common sense to perceive that the idea of such a
being is an idea without object? . . . Does it, at least, require more
than common sense to realize that it is folly and madness for men
to hate and torment one another about unintelligible opinions concerning
a being of this kind? In short, does not everything prove that morality
and virtue are totally incompatible with the notions of a God, whom
his ministers and interpreters have described, in every country, as the
most capricious, unjust and cruel of tyrants, whose pretended will,
however, must serve as law and rule to the inhabitants of the earth?

27

*   *   *

Theologians repeatedly tell us that God is infinitely just, but that *his justice is not the justice of man.* Of what kind or nature then is this divine justice? What idea can I form of a justice, which so often resembles injustice? Is it not to confound all ideas of just and unjust, to say that what is equitable in God is iniquitous in his creatures? How can we receive for our model a being, whose divine virtues are precisely the opposite of human virtues?

Albert Camus

From the moment that man submits God to moral judgment, he kills Him in his own heart. And then what is the basis of morality? God is denied in the name of justice, but can the idea of justice be understood without the idea of God? At this point are we not in the realm of absurdity? Absurdity is the concept that Nietszche meets face to face. In order to be able to dismiss it, he pushes it to extremes: morality is the ultimate aspect of God, which must be destroyed before reconstruction can begin. Then God no longer exists and is no longer responsible for our existence; man must resolve to act, in order to exist.

Antony Flew

Once upon a time two explorers came upon a clearing in the jungle. In the clearing were growing many flowers and many weeds. One explorer says, "Some gardener must tend this plot." The other disagrees, "There is no gardener." So they pitch their tents and set a watch. No gardener. . . . So they set up a barbed wire fence. They electrify it. They patrol with bloodhounds . . . But no shrieks even suggest that some intruder has received a shock. No movements of the wire ever betray an invisible climber. The bloodhounds never give cry. Yet still the Believer is not convinced. "But there is a gardener, invisible, intangible, insensible to electric shocks, a gardener who has no scent and makes no sound, a gardener who comes secretly to look after the garden which he loves." At last the Skeptic despairs, "But what remains of your original assertion? Just how does what you call an invisible, intangible, eternally elusive gardener differ from an imaginary gardener or even no gardener at all?"

A. Eustace Haydon

More needful than faith in God is faith that man can give love, justice, peace, and all his beloved moral values embodiment in human relations. Denial of this faith is the only real atheism. Without it, belief in all the galaxies of gods is mere futility. With it, and the practice that flows from it, man need not mourn the passing of the gods.

*   *   *

The biography of a god can be written only as a phase of the life process of a people. . . .

Gods who have won a secure place in the gratitude of their worshippers for services rendered, grow most easily by enlarging their powers in response to still unsatisfied desires. The unattained always calls to man from beyond the horizon. . . . From the earliest ages he has loaded responsibility upon his heavenly friends to do for him what he could not do for himself, and the gods have graciously bowed to bear the burden.

Julian Huxley

What are the changes which would inevitably flow from . . . reclaiming from the idea of God that garment of personality which we have put upon it, and at the same time possessing our souls in patience and not asserting that we know what we cannot know. They would be many and diverse. First and foremost, the thinking world would see, with a sigh of profound relief, the cutting of that Gordian knot of which man has tied up the absolute goodness and omnipotence of God with the evil of the world. This has always been a stumbling-block to belief. When natural catastrophes occur and we see thousands of innocent men suffer from no cause, as in the earthquake of Messina or the Mississippi floods; when diseases strike blindly right and left, like the influenza epidemic of 1918, with its ten million victims, or the Plague of London in 1665, or in India today; when we see children born deformed, deaf, blind, or crippled to a life of suffering or hardship; or an idiot child produced by the best of married couples; when we see the success of men who are cruel, unscrupulous, or definitely wicked, and the hard lot of others who are industrious and upright; most of all when we are confronted with a gigantic catastrophe, like the War, in which not blind outer nature, but our own human nature is involved, and man's best impulses, of devotion, courage, intellect, endurance, self-sacrifice, pity, are all in one way or another employed upon the task of killing other men by thousands and tens of thousands—then it is difficult for many to believe in a personal God. . . .

But if God be one name for the Universe as it impinges on our lives and makes part of our thoughts, then the horror and the contradiction is lifted. Wars remain; unmerited disease and suffering remain; catastrophes remain; but the problems which they present, which may all be summed up as the problem of evil, are no longer the same. They are no longer problems of a divine morality for which no problems should exist, but of the ultimate nature of the Universe. The Mississippi floods are terrible; but they are not divine vengeance which ruins the innocent with the guilty. Bubonic plague or influenza will not be stayed with prayers; they are appalling, but they may be controlled by taking thought and taking pains. Volcanic eruptions and earthquakes may not be preventable, but they may often be foretold. At least they do not point an accusing finger at Heaven and a Ruler of Heaven responsible for them. Best of all, most stimulating of all, is the change when we come to human evil, the evil which is evil in essence as well as in effect, the evil of those who might have done good. . . .

The release of God from the anthropomorphic disguise of personality also provides release from that vice which may be termed Providentialism. God provides for the sparrow, we are told; how much more for man? And so this beneficent power will always provide. Divine Providence is an excuse for the poor whom we have always with us; for the human improvidence which produces whole broods of children without reflection or care as to how they shall live; for not taking action when we are lazy; or, more rarely, for justifying the action we do take when we are energetic. From the point of view of the future destiny of man, the present is a time of clash between the idea of providentialism and the idea of humanism— human control by human effort in accordance with human ideals. If providentialism wins, humanity is doomed either to stagnation or else to distortion, the material and the spiritual sides of his life being in disharmony. And in spite of the old proverb, "the Gods help them who help themselves," the conception of a personal divine being is the chief asset on the side of Providentialism.

Protagoras

Man is a measure of all things, of things that are, that they are; and of things that are not, that they are not. . . . With regard to the gods I know not whether they exist or not or what they are like. Many things prevent our knowing; the subject is obscure, and brief is the span of mortal life.

Robert Green Ingersoll

Would an infinitely wise, good, and powerful God, intending to produce man, commence with the lowest possible forms of life; with the simplest organism that can be imagined, and, during immeasurable periods of time, slowly and almost imperceptibly improve upon the rude beginning, until man was evolved? Would countless ages thus be wasted in the production of awkward forms, afterwards abandoned? Can the intelligence of man discover the least wisdom in covering the earth with crawling, creeping horrors, that live only upon the agonies and pangs of others? Can we see the propriety of so constructing the earth that only an insignificant portion of its surface is capable of producing an intelligent man? Who can appreciate the mercy of so making the world that all animals devour animals; so that every mouth is a slaughterhouse, and every stomach a tomb? Is it possible to discover infinite intelligence and love in universal and eternal carnage?

What would we think of a father who should give a farm to his children, and before giving them possession should plant upon it thousands of deadly shrubs and vines; should stock it with ferocious beasts and poisonous reptiles; should take pains to put a few swamps in the neighbourhood to breed malaria; should so arrange matters that the ground would occasionally open and swallow a few of his darlings; and, besides all this, should establish a few volcanoes in the immediate vicinity, that might at any moment overwhelm his children with rivers of fire? Suppose that this father neglected to tell his children which of the plants were deadly; that the reptiles were poisonous; failed to say anything about the earthquakes, and kept the volcano business a profound secret; would we pronounce him angel or fiend?

And yet this is exactly what the orthodox God has done. . . .

Each nation has created a god, and the god has always resembled his creators. He hated and loved what they hated and loved, and he was invariably found on the side of those in power. Each god was intensely patriotic, and detested all nations but his own.

None of these gods could give a true account of the creation of this little earth. All were woefully deficient in geology and astronomy. As a rule they were most miserable legislators, and as executives they were far inferior to the average of American presidents.

No god was ever in advance of the nation that created him. The Negroes represented their deities with black skins and curly hair. The Mongolians gave to theirs a yellow complexion and dark almond-shaped eyes.

There may be a God who will make us happy in another world. If he does, it will be more than he has accomplished in this. A being who has the power to prevent it and yet allows thousands and millions of his children to starve, who devours them with earthquakes, who allows whole nations to be enslaved, cannot—in my judgment—be implicitly depended upon to do justice in another world.

Arthur Schopenhauer

Against Pantheism I have chiefly this objection only, that it says nothing. To call the world God is not to explain it, but only to enrich language with a superfluous synonym of the word "world."

Mark Twain

Strange, indeed, that you should not have suspected that your universe and its contents were only dreams, visions, fiction! Strange, because they are so frankly and hysterically insane—like all dreams: A God who could make good children as easily as bad, yet preferred to make bad ones; who could have made everyone of them happy, yet never made a single happy one; who made them prize their bitter life, yet stingily cut it short; who gave his angels painless lives, yet cursed his other children with biting miseries and maladies of mind and body; who mouths justice and invented hell—mouths mercy and

invented hell—mouths Golden Rules, and forgiveness multiplied by
seventy times seven, and invented hell; who mouths morals to other
people and has none himself; who frowns upon crimes, yet commits
them all; who created man without invitation, then tries to shuffle
the responsibility for man's acts upon man, instead of honorably
placing it where it belongs, upon himself; and finally, with altogether
divine obtuseness, invites this poor, abused slave to worship him!

Humanism

Gina Allen

I first saw the light one night when I was sixteen years old. It was intially a very small light—the beam from the flashlight that enabled me to read under the bedcovers when I was supposed to be sleeping. That night I was reading a Little Blue Book that had been given to me by my boyfriend. It was Percy Bysshe Shelley's *The Necessity of Atheism.*

I usually say that until the moment I opened the book I was a very religious young woman, but I suppose I had actually been outgrowing my religion for a while. For one thing, my boyfriend, a freethinker, had been giving me books like this and had been making me defend my religious beliefs—which I had difficulty doing to his satisfaction, and my own.

So I was prepared for Shelley and his atheism even though I didn't know it. And, as I read, the light got brighter and brighter. Not from the flashlight I was reading with but from my mind absorbing what I read. Shelley's logic shattered, in one memorable night, all the Sunday school lessons, Bible studies, and sermons I had been exposed to for years.

My first reaction was fury, a fury so strong that I risked confronting my father the next morning at breakfast. "You can't possibly believe all that god stuff! Do you?" I demanded. "You're an intelligent, educated man. God is as much a hoax as Santa Claus and not nearly as much fun. And only kids believe in Santa."

His response made me even angrier. This pillar of the religious community, this trustee of the local Presbyterian church, this man who supported the church financially and attended services every Sunday told me calmly that no, he didn't believe what the church

35

taught. But he did believe that without the church there would be no morality in the world. Children learned right and wrong in the church, and adults lived righteous lives because they believed in God and heaven and hell.

I have since learned that this attitude is not unusual among many who appear to be religious. They are less concerned with their own spirituality than with the conduct of others. They see themselves as superior, able to understand their religion as mythology and still conduct their lives morally. But they don't think the ordinary person can do that, so they count on religion to keep the masses under control. Indeed, throughout history such "superior" men have used religion to regulate their slaves and subjugate women.

In my first heady release from religion I too thought it was the only thing that had kept me "good." My life would change: I could sin. As a teenager, for me the three great sins were smoking, drinking, and premarital sex.

I told my boyfriend that I had seen the light. He was glad. He said he thought I was too intelligent to stay caught up in religion forever. Then I told him that we could sin together. We could drink, and smoke, and have sex. He looked at me as if I were crazy. I could do those things if I wished, he said, but he was in training. As captain of the high-school football team, a star basketball player, and a Golden Gloves boxer, he was always in training.

He wasn't "good" because he believed in a god but because he wanted to be an athlete. Slowly it dawned on me that I hadn't been "good" because I believed in a god but because I loved my family and friends, enjoyed my studies and my music, and wanted to prepare myself for all life's possibilities.

I have never, ever regretted the night I saw the light. I shall be ever grateful to the young athlete who gave me that Little Blue Book (and to Emanuel Haldeman-Julius, the publisher of Little Blue Books). I have stopped being personally furious with the Christian religion that duped me as a child, but I continue to be alarmed at religion when it hurts people, stunts their growth, and practices sexism and racism.

When I visit my family I go to church with them. I cringe through the Apostles' Creed. How narrow and restrictive it is! I cringe through the hymns, too. I'm a pacifist, so "Onward Christian Soldiers" is repugnant. And "Amazing Grace"—which asks God "to save a wretch like me"—shows how destructive religion can be of self-esteem. It spreads guilt instead of joy. It denies nature and closes minds to scientific knowledge.

So except for an annual journey back to my roots in family and the Presbyterian church, I have not returned to religion, nor have I missed it. My associates since the night I saw the light have been people with whom I share common interests and goals, people trying to make this world better, not hoping for heaven. Like Abou Ben Adhem, in Leigh Hunt's wise poem, they are moral because they love this earth and those with whom they share it. I trust they can say the same about me.

H. J. Blackham

Humanism is a concept of man. There are many such concepts and men have not agreed about them, and are not likely to for some time to come. I would distinguish between a concept of human nature, which might be a synthesis of relevant knowledge on which general agreement could be expected and worked for, and concepts of man which go beyond information—as Humanism does.

Many concepts of man have been therapeutic: man is sick, not his true self, in the sense that he is "fallen" (Christianity), "earthbound" (Hinduism, Buddhism), "empirically worthless" (Hegel), "alienated" (Marxism), "inauthentic" (existentialism). In each case there is a justifying total view and a dependent strategy for living: man becomes his true self by obedience to the divine will, by conformity to the cosmic design, by identification with Being or with historical process, by assuming his autonomy in the continuous exercise of choice. Some of these concepts are historical, some metaphysical; some are centered in the cosmos, some in the Creator, some in man himself or in a transaction in which he is partner. All have sophisticated traditions that make these abrupt references look like ones of a caricature.

Humanism too has a long tradition. It is historical rather than metaphysical (and therefore Western rather than Eastern), and it is centered in man but is distinct in being neither therapeutic nor dualistic.

It is less ready to differentiate between what man is and what he ought to be and refuses to define him in terms of a universal given end. This is by no means because of complacency about man and his future. Rather, it is because of a sensitive regard for each man as his own end and for man as responsible for man. This notion of human responsibility is the nuclear idea in the definition of Humanism. There is no entelechy, no built-in pattern of perfection. Man is his own rule and his own end. Human life is in human hands. The strategy for living is "adopt and adapt," not "obey" or "conform."

This view is both prescriptive and unprescriptive. It is prescriptive in being a concept of man and a strategy for living; unprescriptive in leaving ends open. As Nietzsche observed, if man is totally responsible and there is no built-in order, if ends are open and history is merely "a great index of human possibilities," everything is permissible. Here Humanism is the human decision to give moral equivalence to all men as human beings. Acceptance of interdependence and the solidarity of interests as the basis of human relations means acceptance of a share in joint responsibility for creating for all the conditions of a life worthy to be called human, a human providence in which each may be his own end without mockery.

Thus Humanism calls man to a human program. The main features of this program are familiar: international security, aid, conservation, population control, development and direction of technology, education for autonomy and an open society. Such a formidable global program is liable to leave the ordinary Humanist, who is trying to make a living, slightly defeatist or cynical. Here is Humanist faith, a reasonable faith in intelligent action. The character of the program is such that its call comes home to everyone's possibilities to respond.

On the basis of this interdependence, there remains the inalienable responsibility of each for himself as his own end. It is the glory of Humanism that here it is unprescriptive but may be exemplary. Personal life is choice not obligation, a work of art not a set task, an offering not a requirement, a creation not a prize.

Abstractly, then, Humanism is a concept of man focused upon a program for humanity. Concretely, it is my idea of, and my commitment to, my part in that program, which includes not least the life that is in my own hands.

Joseph L. Blau

Consider, for a moment, an acorn. We may say that it has a natural end: to become an oak tree. We may add that this natural end includes the perpetuation of its species. The acorn is not conscious of its end. We should not speak, for instance, of the end as purposed, nor of the acorn as motivated by self- or species-preservation. The realization of its end (its natural teleology, in Aristotelian terms) is an unfolding of latencies, not an ethical striving.

Again, consider a boar. Once more, we may say that it has an end: self-preservation, and thereby the perpetuation of its species. Realization of the natural end of the boar, however, may preclude realization of the natural end of the acorn. But the boar is conscious neither of its own end nor of how it frustrates the acorn's. The boar does not have a purpose that motivates it to eat acorns in order to prevent their developing into oak trees. The boar has instincts that impel it to eat acorns to fulfil its natural teleology. It does not consider its own welfare, still less the welfare of the acorn. A boar cannot be judged ethically.

Now let us turn to the human species. Man, too, has a natural end, even as has a boar or an acorn. In a sense, his natural end is as fundamentally decisive for him as is the natural end of an acorn or a boar. To the extent that this is so, that the human being is a creature of his nature, the human *telos* is self- and species-preservation. But members of the human race are conscious of their natural end and are, therefore, in a position to judge means as contributory or noncontributory to this end. The reservoir of means that have been judged contributory is the culture of humankind.

Human culture includes science (what humanity has found out about its surroundings) as well as ethics (what humanity has found out about its internal relations). Science, we say, is self-corrective; the continued application of those very techniques that have led to incorrect or inadequate judgments about human surroundings will lead to the correction and reformulation of these judgments. We do not recognize or sufficiently stress that ethics, too, is self-corrective. As time goes on, humankind has reformulated many erroneous earlier ethical judgments in accordance with the results of increased ethical awareness. These changes are slower than those resulting from the self-corrective method of science, and at some times in the history of mankind the chasm between human knowledge and its application to the ethical relations of persons and groups seems unbridgeable.

Human culture includes art (the concrete expression of human ideals in plastic forms) as well as ethics (the abstract expression of human ideals in the form of principles). In either form, the human activity of projecting ideals as goals is purposive. For the human species, ends are transformed into targets. This is not the case in the rest of the range of natural being, from acorn and boar to yak and zebra. Humankind transforms even its natural end into a purposed goal. It strives consciously toward the improvement of its own species, not merely toward its perpetuation. Individual members of the species, in seeking self-improvement, attempt to apply general ethical principles to the re-creation of themselves as works of art and thus the members can contribute purposively to the improvement of the human species.

The acorn in its unfolding cares not in the least whether boar or human survives or perishes. The boar in its blind lust for survival is unconcerned with the fate of human or acorn. Human purposes, however, can and often do include care and concern for oaks and boars insofar as the survival, and, indeed, the improvement, of oaks and boars contribute to the realization of human ends. Only recently have human science, art and ethics come to know how profoundly implicated in human welfare are oaks and boars and other natural beings, and we see already a shifting of human goals toward more pervasive ecological concern.

If, in the vagrant processes of nature, a thinking acorn were to come into being, its philosophy and its religion would be limited by its quercine nature. Its metaphysic would deal with reality from the perspective of the oak; it could not admit the reality of the boar (the boar would be "no thing"). If the artful imaginings of George Orwell's *Animal Farm* were to occur in nature and thinking boars come into being, their philosophy and religion would be restricted by their nature's conceiving of all reality as relating to swine. (*Quercianism* and *suidianism* might be appropriate names for these processes.) For us, the case is different. "Man," said Diderot, "is the single place from which we must begin and to which we must refer everything." But, as we have seen, human reality includes oaks and boars as well as people. Human imagination can "take the role of the other" even when that other is not human. Human good can include the good of oaks and swine. "*Homo sum,*" said Terence, "I am a human being; I regard nothing of human concern as alien to me."

This is Humanism, a philosophy as natural to humankind as quercianism to the acorn or suidianism to the boar. It is an ethical philosophy because it sets forth principled goals for self- and species-improvement. It is grounded in human culture, and therefore rests on both art and science. It is an inclusive philosophy, for better oaks and better swine are incorporated into its quest for the betterment of humankind.

Miriam Allen deFord

It is perhaps unfortunate that the term *Humanism* was ever adopted for a humanity-centered philosophy; the word had already had a long and honorable career as denominating the renewed interest in the ancient classics and the humanities that came with the Renaissance. *Rationalism* or *secularism* would have been much more precise. Either of them, of course, would have barred the religiously-oriented, but that, in my opinion, would have been desirable rather than disadvantageous.

However, as the American association took over that word in 1933 and as it has been more or less accepted also by our British colleagues, exact definitions have become necessary.

My own tentative general definition of *Humanism* as a whole would be that it is a philosophical system based on the concept that the universe, life, and consequently mankind are the result of natural evolutionary processes alone, and hence that our view of them must be monistic. In other words, there is nothing in existence except random, fortuitous forces which eventually—in the manner of the famous example of the monkeys pounding typewriters who finally emerge with the works of Shakespeare—bring together consonant elements from which under favorable circumstances, galaxies, planetary systems, bacteria and human beings gradually issue and evolve.

Ethical Humanism can best be defined in the words of an anonymous pre-Confucian Chinese philosopher of the tenth century: "Man must look in his own heart to know what he must do." Or, to quote Robert G. Ingersoll, "The accumulated experience of the world is a power and force that works for righteousness. This force is not conscious, not intelligent. It is a result." It is the task of Humanism to show that ethics is a by-product of human experience, not of some supernatural mandate. Man must learn to exercise a high ethical policy toward the earth on which he lives, toward the multitudinous plants and animals inhabiting it with him, toward his fellow humans—yes, and toward himself as well—or cease to survive.

Scientific Humanism in my thinking *is* Humanism; the general definition I have given above predicates a scientific approach to every philosophical, ethical, and intellectual problem. This is not nineteenth-century mechanistic materialism; there are many aspects of proved or provable reality (for example extrasensory perception) that we do not yet understand, but that are still phenomena susceptible to investigation and understanding.

Religious Humanism (*pace* the "liberal religionists") is to me merely a contradiction in terms. Religion in its strict meaning implies belief in nonhumanistic systems, entities, or explanations. A philosophy founded on the agreement that "man is the measure of all things" can have no room for belief in the intervention of nonmaterial postulates. Conceivably, one might say that a person who believes that nothing exists but spirit is as much of a monist as a person who believes that nothing exists but natural, material phenomena. The one thing the adherent to either faith cannot be is a dualist, and religion by any definition is necessarily dependent on a dualistic order.

To put it bluntly and undiplomatically, Humanism, in my viewpoint, must be atheistic or it is not Humanism as I understand it. At the age of thirteen, I concluded that there is sufficient evidence that there are no gods, there is no soul, and there is no survival of personality after death. That was seventy-one years ago, and I have never heard any arguments since to cause me to negate that conclusion. I presume, in view of the wide orbit of belief among members of the American Humanist Association, that this makes me a heretical Humanist; nevertheless, as long as the orbit remains wide enough to include me, I shall still claim membership.

Albert Ellis

Do I personally participate in theistic religious commitments, prayer, devotion, or ceremony? Definitely not! I believe exactly as much in religious commitment—and the prayer, devotion, and ritual that normally accompany it—as I do in commitment to Santa Claus and my fairy godmother. My life is so joyously replete with devotion (but not devoutness) to psychology, psychotherapy, sexology, marriage and family relations, writing, composing rational humorous songs, teaching, supervising, directing a nonprofit therapeutic institute, personal loves and friendships, and many other active interests that I would be pretty stupid to waste any of my valuable time devoting myself to religious ceremonies or praying to mythical gods.

I can safely say that I respect many people, things, and ideas—but I am highly allergic to *worshiping* anything, even my own creation, rational-emotive therapy (RET). I am strongly committed to its theory and practice, but I sincerely hope I'm not a reverent, "masturbatory" RETer! I distinctly *prefer* my system of therapy to other systems and clearly want it to prevail. But I never think of it as a dogma that *has* to succeed.

To be sure, as a psychotherapist and theorist I have come to think that excessive reverence and worship lead to unhealthy mental states.

As I wrote in an essay called "The Case Against Religiosity": "It is my contention that pietistic theists and religionists—virtually all people imbued with intense religiosity and fanaticism—are emotionally disturbed: usually neurotic but sometimes psychotic. For they strongly and rigidly believe in the same kinds of profound irrationalities, absolutistic musts, and unconditional necessities in which seriously disturbed people powerfully believe. When, moreover, they employ the logico-empirical methods of science, and when they fully accept (while often distinctly disliking and actively trying to change) reality, they are able to surrender their devoutness and to become significantly less disturbed. Indeed, I hypothesize, the more scientific, open-minded, and straight-thinking about themselves, about others, and about the world people are, the less neurotically they will think, feel, and behave. This is my major hypothesis about the relationship between absolutistic religious belief (religiosity) and mental health. The evidence that I have found, clinically and experimentally, in support of this hypothesis (as well as the evidence falsifying the hypothesis that devout religiosity is significantly correlated with and probably causative of good mental health) seems to be most impressive."

Since I have been intimately involved with more than ten thousand psychotherapy clients over the past forty-three years, and since I have taught, supervised, lectured, and given RET workshops to about a quarter of a million more students of psychology and self-help procedures, I have an exceptionally wide acquaintanceship with "normal" and "disturbed" individuals. Of these many people, I know literally thousands who do not believe in God or the supernatural and who do not practice a formal religion but who definitely lead exemplary (and often truly outstanding) lives. I also, of course, know hundreds of theists who have been happy helping themselves and others; but my (perhaps biased) impression is that the happiest and most productive people I know are much more frequently in the nontheistic than in the theistic class.

Lack of religious worship, prayer, and ceremony has affected my life very favorably—by giving me much more time than I otherwise would have had to be committed to other, quite worldly pursuits. Including personal pleasure!

I consider life meaningful even though I reject the idea of a theistic being, because I make sure that I always *give* it real meaning. I agree with Jean-Paul Sartre that, in themselves, life and the universe are meaningless and absurd—have no intrinsic meaning or value whatsoever. Only humans and our humanism *create* personal and world significance.

My life, I fully intend, will be highly meaningful till the day I die, because I am determined to always *make* it so. How? In many ways. But mainly by being as kind as I can be to others—and, notably, to myself!

Edward L. Ericson

Ethical Humanism is a philosophy and moral faith founded upon the twin principles of human responsibility and personal worth. While uniformity of belief is not characteristic of Ethical Humanists, most affirm moral responsibility (based upon the assumption of freedom of choice) as a genuine human capacity that education, religion, and the social order must seek to maximize.

Authentic moral freedom derives from the nature and creative activity of man himself, from the interplay of his social feeling and rationality (the ability to foresee consequences and consider conflicting ends) combined with the drive to achieve meaning and wholeness in personal and social life. Thus, man is a goal-seeking organism whose values can never be treated as purely arbitrary or accidental, however conflicted or distorted they may be, since they arise from needs and relationships grounded in the realities of human life and history.

Moral problems are therefore *real* problems; man's dignity, as William James saw, consists in his fighting what he rightly experiences as a real battle over genuine moral stakes. The substantial and rational character of our deepest and most enduring values enables the Ethical Humanist to live in the rational belief that he is dealing with goods that are objective without the further claim of their being absolute, and that are relative (relational) without the false inference of their being merely subjective. The Ethical Humanist finds his "golden mean" in an earth-born, life-centered and realistic ethic—open, empathic, pragmatic, and nonexclusive—enabling us to avoid the extremes of absolutism and nihilism, which are alike corrosive of meaningful freedom and responsibility.

Ethical Humanist views are held widely among educators, religious liberals, secularists, and theorists of democratic life. Especially the philosophical heirs and successors of William James, F. C. S. Schiller, John Dewey, Morris R. Cohen, and related thinkers subscribe to variations of the same outlook.

As social thinkers and activists, Ethical Humanists stress an ethic that emphasizes the interdependence of cultural and social systems, the quality of races and the values of open political and spiritual interchange. All subscribe to the use of democratic methods and the avoidance of authoritarian and terrorist means, whether exploited by left or right, which break down the relationships and trust upon which mutual help and civilized standards rest.

As the ideological battleline has shifted from the now largely moribund claims of fundamentalist and authoritarian religion to the sanguinary assaults of political totalitarianism upon liberal values and standards, Ethical Humanists have become increasingly able to work with democratic and progressive churchmen, as with secular educators and reformers, to effect social change within the orderly processes of constitutional democracy. The future of this irenic and mediatory ethic, like so much else of humanistic value in civilization, hinges upon the efficacy of orderly and democratic procedures as instruments of social reconstruction.

Sidney Hook

Definitions of Humanism should avoid the pitfall of so defining it that it excludes no one. If the Holy Grail is everywhere there is no point in its quest! For example, in an otherwise historically scholarly article in the *Encyclopaedia of Philosophy* [ed. Paul Edwards, New York, Macmillan, 1967] we are told that: "Humanism is also any philosophy which recognizes the value or dignity of man and makes him the measure of all things or somehow [*sic!*] takes human nature, its limits, or its interests as its theme." Surely this is too broad! It catches almost everyone in its far-flung net. Who denies the value of man? Not even the Torquemadas of this world. Since *both* Protagoras and Socrates are Humanists, it is not necessary to make the view that man is the measure of all things a necessary element in the definition of Humanism. It would exclude not only Socrates but atheistic Humanists like Bertrand Russell and Morris R. Cohen to whom the Protagorean dictum was anathema. To them, the proposition that man is the measure of all things is an expression of self-defeating subjectivity.

As a first step towards clarification of issues and standpoints,

I should like to propose that Humanism today be regarded primarily as an *ethical* doctrine and movement. We already have a term in use, the connotations of which embrace what is generally meant by "scientific Humanism"—namely, "naturalism."

There are Humanists who are naturalists (John Dewey), Humanists who are supernaturalists (like William James), and Humanists who are non-naturalists (like Felix Adler and G. E. Moore). These men differ not in their chief ethical values but in their meta-ethical analysis of the meanings and justification of the "good" and the "right."

Religion, as a system of overbeliefs about the existence of God and related views, I regard as a *private* matter. So long as I am not requested to give it any public support or affirmation, I have no more desire to expose, refute, or confound it than I do my neighbor's belief that his wife is the most beautiful woman in the world. (The "truth" is, of course, that mine is!) I have grown weary of being told that my "concern" with human freedom or the "fire in my heart" that blazes up when I hear of human cruelty is evidence of my religious nature.

Abstractly, except when two terms are exhaustive and exclusive of the alternatives, it is absurd to define a term by its negations, for such definition does not distinguish it from other terms in an indeterminedly large universe of discourse. But in specific, historical contexts sometimes we can make progress towards an adequate definition when we stress what we want to exclude. . . .

If I had to propose a short positive definition on the basis of these negations, I would say that an *Ethical Humanist today is one who relies on the arts of intelligence to defend, enlarge, and enhance the areas of human freedom in the world* [italics added]. Ethical Humanists may differ from each other, but they respect those with whom they disagree. They are not fanatics of virtue. They recognize that good conflicts with good, right with right, and sometimes the good with the right. To these conflicts they bring the only value that is also the judge of its own efficacy and limitation—human intelligence.

Paul Kurtz

Humanists have been debating for years the proper definition of Humanism. It is clear that Humanism is not a dogma or creed and that there are many varieties of, and meanings given to, Humanism. Nevertheless, one may suggest at least four characteristics that contemporary Humanists emphasize.

First, Humanists have some confidence in man and they believe that the only bases for morality are human experience and human needs. Second, many or most Humanists are opposed to all forms of supernaturalistic and authoritarian religion. Third, many Humanists believe that scientific intelligence and critical reason can assist in reconstructing our moral values. And fourth, Humanism is humanitarian in that it is concerned with the good life and social justice as moral ideals.

Humanism as a movement is wide enough to include many people who will agree with some of the above points, but not all. What characterizes an increasing number of people is a commitment to a moral point of view in which mankind is viewed as a whole. Such a characteristic does not make one a Humanist by itself. Yet, it is an ideal that most Humanists share. Humanists may honestly disagree about their political beliefs and about many social questions. There is no Humanist party line. What Humanists today share in common, however, are a concern for humanity, a belief that moral values must be removed from the mantle of theological dogma, and a conviction that our moral ideals must be constantly re-examined and revised in the light of present needs and social demands.

Secular Humanism

Paul Kurtz

One thing that has become evident is the need to emphasize new directions for Humanism. Although its opponents credit Secular Humanism with dominating modern society, Humanists often consider themselves to be dissenters and iconoclasts, rejecting many of the sacred cows of society. Humanists have long been critical of fundamentalist religious institutions and beliefs, particularly when they are imposed upon society. Humanists have long argued for the freedom to develop conscience outside the context of a theistic world view, the tolerance of diverse life styles, and the separation of church and state. There has been a continuous struggle between a theistic view, in which only God can save mankind, and the naturalistic scientific one, in which humans must seek their own solutions. Radically different moral conceptions have flowed from these different views of the universe. Regretfully, in these days of revivalism, all too few in the community, the press, or the media are willing to risk attacking biblical indoctrination.

Sometimes Humanists are identified with liberalism or radicalism, especially when they are critics of the social order and are working for reform. Other times they are viewed as conservative apologists for the status quo, as when they defend civil liberties or reject so-called "progressive" solutions that may do more harm than good. The salient point is that Humanism is committed to free inquiry. Its first principle is to use reason and critical intelligence in testing claims to truth or morality and in modifying beliefs and principles, even the most cherished ones, in the light of their consequences. Humanists are wont to expose the gullibility of others and point out the fallibility of human judgment. They are willing to engage

49

in controversy when they believe it has social merit, for truth is often discovered in the give and take of critical debate.

This sometimes leads friends as well as adversaries of Humanism to mistakenly infer that Humanism is basically negative. Key questions must be raised: Does Secular Humanism have a constructive role to play? Can it add significantly to the fund of human good? Will Humanism ever supplant the theological or paranormal systems of faith that have no foundation in fact? Can Humanism provide "spiritual" sustenance and transcending ideals that can stir conviction and commitment? Does life have genuine meaning, and is it worth living? Does Humanism represent a viable alternative for society? Can it present significant options?

The Humanist believes that the answers to these questions can be in the *affirmative* and that the Humanist moral outlook is *positive.* Humanism emphasizes creative fulfillment as the end of life; it is committed to the shared joys of family life, love, work, and career. The Humanist wishes to maximize individual freedom and to create a society in which the widest degree of autonomy of choice is present. Humanists have been sympathetic to libertarianism, insofar as it cultivates the conditions that enable individuals to develop and excel. Humanism is not to be equated with irresponsible hedonism; it expresses a genuine moral concern. It is not self-centered or egoistic, but has consistently encouraged an appreciation for the needs of others. This entails the basic ethical principles of democracy: equality and fairness. Humanists have sought to extend this compassionate concern not only to their relatives and neighbors within the same community, but to the entire community of humankind. The ideal is to consider humanity as a whole.

The critics of Humanism vehemently maintain that Humanism is unable to provide an adequate justification for moral obligation and responsibility, but Humanists deny this. Moral decisions may be tested objectively by reference to their consequences in action. Ethics is autonomous, and any effort to deduce morality from religion or theology loses the distinctive qualities of the moral experience. Historically, in any case, religious believers have not been demonstrably more ethical than nonbelievers.

That is one reason why Humanists have argued that moral education be taught in the schools. In promoting moral development, or values clarification, the teacher is not necessarily imposing on students the "religion of Secular Humanism." We believe both in the separation of church and state and in the neutrality of the schools. Ethical inquiry is as old as Western civilization itself and is a field of learning, like mathematics or history, that should be taught.

Yet the question is raised: Can Secular Humanism itself—free of any illusions about human destiny—provide sufficient inspiration for individuals, for young people adrift, for those seeking purpose in life, for average people who hunger for a deeper meaning to human experience? This is the issue that secular humanism must confront directly: Can Humanism help open doors so that individuals, singly and in cooperation with others, can create lives that are rich in enjoyment, eloquent, and meaningful? Humanism as a general philosophical outlook is surely much broader in influence than institutionalized Humanism; yet the ultimate test of a philosophical perspective is its relevance to *praxis,* to the concrete experiences of human beings as they are lived.

I have no easy answers about whether Secular Humanism—which many of the intellectual leaders of our day believe to be an appropriate alternative—will eventually succeed in fashioning symbols and ideals that can inspire commitment and dedication in the ordinary person. Yet it is a decisive challenge. Whether Secular Humanism will continue as a force in the civilization of the future will depend on how well it can respond to this need.

PART II

Death and Immortality

Death and Immortality

Ingersoll once observed, "Immortality comes from no religion but nearly every religion comes from the desire for personal immortality." Humanists accept this distinction. Accepting the reality of mortality is a feature that distinguishes Humanists from the overwhelming majority of the orthodox, traditional Judeo-Christian communicants and many Eastern religion worshippers. Along with the absence of a concept of "God," the acceptance of personal mortality is a unique and distinguishing characteristic of Humanism. From these two basic premises of naturalistic Humanism, numerous other concepts are derived and serve to characterize contemporary Humanist thought. At the same time, Humanists can speak honestly and embrace several authentic views of immortality. Certainly Shakespeare, St. Joan, and Mozart live on in the hearts and minds of far more people today than were aware of them during their lifetimes. There is the immortality of the indestructible human personality and his or her contributions. In addition, for those who propagate the species, there is biological immortality. How often we hear it said, "He is the spitting image of his father," or "She certainly reminds me of her mother when she was a teenager!"

In fact, some Humanists insist that a primary function of today's Humanism is to keep alive the memories and messages of yesterday's great benefactors of Humanism and the human race. If we view Humanism as a dynamic continuum, it behooves each and every contemporary Humanist to be knowledgeable about our past, the great spokespeople, and their contributions.

Historically, religion has been preoccupied with the impossible task of seeking to outwit death. The question that Humanists ask is not, "Do we live again? Am I, are we, immortal?" No, Humanists ask, "Is there authentic life before death?" Can we become inner-directed, self-motivated responsible individuals, here and now, and in the absence of any ultimate reward and punishment mechanism associated with traditional faiths? If Humanists succeed in promoting decency, dignity, and dedication to the highest values in life for their sake (and humanity's benefit), it will, indeed, be a historic first. The basic premise in religion has been the promise of eternal residence in Heaven for the faithful and in Hell for the faithless. Humanism does not offer this but suggests, instead, that Heaven lies in the quality of life we fashion here and now, on this our maiden and only voyage.

Immortality

Corliss Lamont

One of man's chief answers to the onslaught of death is to envisage those enduring things which outlive the brevities and vicissitudes of this-earthly existence. The commonest form of this imaginative embodiment of everlastingness has been the belief in a supernatural personal immortality beyond the grave. But there have always been a number of men and women who have realized the wholly mythical nature of the idea of a future life. They have transferred the powerful urge to partake of eternity to such concepts as those of biological immortality through one's children and descendants, of social immortality through the impact of one's work or fame, and of material or chemical immortality through the indestructibility of the elements of the body.

If the natural and usually egoistic tendency of men towards self-perpetutation can be sublimated into the desire for biological or social immortality, it is a real step forward. While our prophets of ultimate doom, today often scientists rather than theologians, predict that at some date in the very distant future this earth will become uninhabitable and the living creatures upon it extinguished, there is at least a chance that developments in science and social cooperation will be able to prevent such an outcome. In any case we can be sure that great Nature itself is eternal and that in its infinite space and infinite time it possesses the unceasing potentiality of creations far more significant than man.

These speculations, however, are perhaps rather irrelevant in view of the fact that our astrophysicists foresee a livable earth for millions and even billions of years hence. The progress and well-being of humanity through such vast tracts of time is assuredly a broad enough and noble enough aim to maintain the moral idealism of those who insist that permanence over the ages is essential to make human values worthwhile.

Robert Green Ingersoll

It may be that man lives forever, and it may be that what we call life ends with what we call death. I have had no experience beyond the grave, and very little back of birth. Consequently, I cannot say that I have a belief on this subject. I can simply say that I have no knowledge on this subject, and know of no fact in nature that I would use as the corner-stone of a belief.

Thucydides

The whole earth is the tomb of heroic men and their story is not graven only on stone over their clay but abides everywhere without visible symbol, woven into the stuff of other men's lives.

H. L. Mencken

Life is pleasant and I have enjoyed it, but I have no yearning to clutter up the Universe after it is over.

John Stuart Mill

The only part of the conduct of anyone, for which he is amenable to society, is that which concerns others. In the part which merely concerns himself, his independence is, of right, absolute. Over himself, over his own body and mind, the individual is sovereign.

George Eliot

The Choir Invisible

Oh may I join the choir invisible
Of those immortal dead who live again
In minds made better by their presence: live
In pulses stirred to generosity,
In deeds of daring rectitude, in scorn
For miserable aims that end with self,
In thoughts sublime that pierce the night like stars,
And with their mild persistence urge man's search
To vaster issues.
         So to live is heaven:
To make undying music in the world,
Breathing as beauteous order that controls
With growing sway the growing life of man.
So we inherit that sweet purity
For which we struggled, failed, and agonized
With widening retrospect that bred despair.
Rebellious flesh that would not be subdued,
A vicious parent shaming still its child,
Poor anxious penitence, is quick dissolved;
Its discords, quenched by meeting harmonies,
Die in the large and charitable air.
And all our rarer, better, truer self,
That sobbed religiously in yearning song,

That watched to ease the burden of the world,
Laboriously tracing what must be,
And what may yet be better,—saw within
A worthier image for the sanctuary,
And shaped it forth before the multitude,
Divinely human, raising worship so
To higher reverence more mixed with love,—
That better self shall live till human Time
Shall fold its eyelids, and the human sky
Be gathered like a scroll within the tomb
Unread for ever.
           This is life to come,
Which martyred men have made more glorious
For us who strive to follow. May I reach
That purest heaven, be to other souls
The cup of strength in some great agony,
Enkindle generous ardor, feed pure love,
Beget the smiles that have no cruelty,
Be the sweet presence of a good diffused,
And in diffusion ever more intense.
So shall I join the choir invisible
Whose music is the gladness of the world.

Euthanasia

Seneca

You can find men who have gone so far as to profess wisdom and yet maintain that one should not offer violence to one's own life, and hold it accursed for a man to be the means of his own destruction; we should wait, say they, for the end decreed by nature. But one who says this does not see that he is shutting off the path to freedom. The best thing which eternal law ever ordained was that it allowed to us one entrance into life, but many exits. Must I await the cruelty either of disease or of man, when I can depart through the midst of torture, and shake off my troubles? This is the one reason why we cannot complain of life: it keeps no one against his will. Humanity is well situated, because no man is unhappy except by his own fault. Live, if you so desire; if not, you may return to the place whence you came.

Death

Lucretius

A tree cannot exist high in air, or clouds in the depths of the sea, as fish cannot live in the fields, or blood flow in wood or sap in stones. There is a determined and allotted place for the growth and presence of everything. So mind cannot arise alone without body or apart from sinews and blood. . . . You must admit, therefore, that when the body has perished there is an end also of the spirit diffused through it. It is surely crazy to couple a mortal object with an eternal and suppose that they can work in harmony and mutually interact. What can be imagined more incongruous, what more repugnant and discordant, than that a mortal object and one that is immortal and everlasting should unite to form a compound and jointly weather the storms that rage about them?

From all this it follows that *death is nothing to us* and no concern of ours, since our tenure of the mind is mortal. In days of old, we felt no disquiet when the hosts of Carthage poured in to battle on every side—when the whole earth, dizzied by the convulsive shock of war, reeled sickeningly under the high ethereal vault, and between realm and realm the empire of mankind by land and sea trembled in the balance. So, when we shall be no more—when the union of body and spirit that engenders us has been disrupted—to us, who shall then be nothing, nothing by any hazard will happen any more at all. Nothing will have power to stir our senses, not though earth be fused with sea and sea with sky. . . .

If the future holds travail and anguish in store, the self must be in existence, when that time comes, in order to experience it. But from this fate we are redeemed by death, which denies existence to the self that might have suffered these tribulations. Rest assured, therefore, that we have nothing to fear in death. One who no longer is cannot suffer, or differ in any way from one who has never been born, when once this mortal life has been usurped by death the immortal. . . .

The old is always thrust aside to make way for the new, and one thing must be built out of the wreck of another. There is no murky pit of Hell awaiting anyone. There is need of matter, so that later generations may arise; when they have lived out their span, they will all follow you. Bygone generations have taken your road, and those to come will take it no less. So one thing will never cease to spring from another. To none is life given in freehold; to all on lease. Look back at the eternity that passed before we were born, and mark how utterly it counts to us as nothing. This is a mirror that Nature holds up to us, in which we may see the time that shall be after we are dead. Is there anything terrifying in sight—anything depressing—anything that is not more restful than the soundest sleep?

*   *   *

This nature, then, of the soul is protected by the whole body, and is itself the guardian of the body, and the cause of its life; for the two cling together by common roots, and it is seen that they cannot be torn asunder without destruction. Even as it is not easy to tear out the scent from lumps of frankincense, but that its nature too passes away. So it is not easy to draw out the nature of mind and soul from the whole body, but that all alike is dissolved. With first beginnings so closely interlaced from their very birth are they begotten, endowed with a life shared in common, nor, as is clear to see, can the power of body or mind feel apart, either for itself without the force of the other, but by the common motions of the two on this side and on that is sensation kindled and fanned throughout our flesh.

Moreover, the body is never begotten by itself, nor grows alone, nor is seen to last on after death. For never, as the moisture of water often gives off the heat which has been lent to it, and is not for that reason torn asunder itself, but remains unharmed, never, I say, in this way can the abandoned frame bear the separation of the soul, but it utterly perishes torn asunder, and rots away. So from the beginning of existence body and soul in mutual union learn the motions that give life, yea, even when hidden in the mother's limbs and womb, so that separation cannot come to pass without hurt and ruin; so that you can see, since the cause of their life is linked together, that their natures too must be linked in one.

For the rest, if any one is for proving that the body does not feel, and believes that it is the soul mingled with the whole body that takes up this motion, which we call sensation, he is fighting against even plain and true facts. For who will ever tell us what the feeling of the body is, if it be not what the clear fact itself has shown and taught us? "But when the soul has passed away the body is utterly deprived of sensation." Yes, for it loses that which was not its own in life, and many other things besides it loses when it is driven out of life.

Roger E. Greeley

Of all the methods of avoiding or seeking to avoid facing up to your own mortality, supernaturalistic mysticism enjoys great popularity today. It is a last-ditch defense against reason destroying faith in personal immortality. Obfuscation is the battlement behind which mysticism crouches to protect itself, to fend off all attackers.

If an individual says, "I feel at one with the universe"—whatever that may mean—as long as this does not lead to an assumption that because "the universe is eternal, I therefore am also," it is a rather harmless philosophy, I suppose. The problem comes however when such hope replaces hard, honest recognition of the reality of your mortality.

Much of what passes for the "new theology" is but elaborate, circuitous pedantry designed to make immortality, personal immortality both real and beyond the reach of scientific examination.

More than a century ago Ingersoll observed, "Immortality comes from no religion but nearly every religion comes from the desire for personal immortality." No matter how disguised or clothed in pseudo-scientific verbiage supernaturalistic mysticism may be, it is still disposed of by Ingersoll's observation. No matter how we seek to rationalize it, man is mortal and instead of fearing death, we ought to be worrying about not having lived. The Humanist does not ask, "Is there life after death?" but "Is there life *before* death in my own existence and the existence of those I love?"

William Ernest Henley

So Be My Passing

A late lark twitters from the quiet skies;
And from the west,
Where the sun, his day's work ended,
Lingers as in content,
There falls on the old, grey city
An influence luminous and serene,
A shining peace.

The smoke ascends
In a rosy-and-golden haze. The spires
Shine, and are changed. In the valley
Shadows rise. The lark sings on. The sun,
Closing his benediction,
Sinks, and the darkening air
Thrills with a sense of the triumphing night—
Night with her train of stars
And her great gift of sleep.

So be my passing!
My task accomplished and the long day done,
My wages taken, and in my heart
Some late lark singing,
Let me be gathered to the quiet west,
The sundown splendid and serene,
Death.

Albert Camus

Human insurrection, in its exalted and tragic forms, is only, and
can only be, a prolonged protest against death, a violent accusation
against the universal death penalty. In every case that we have come
across, the protest is always directed at everything in creation which
is dissonant, opaque, or promises the solution of continuity. Essentially,
then, we are dealing with a perpetual demand for unity. The rejection
of death, the desire for immortality and for clarity, are the mainsprings
of all these extravagances, whether sublime or puerile. Is it only a
cowardly and personal refusal to die? No, for many of these rebels
have paid the ultimate price in order to live up to their own demands.
The rebel does not ask for life, but for reasons for living. He rejects
the consequences implied by death. If nothing lasts then nothing is
justified; everything that dies is deprived of meaning. To fight against
death amounts to claiming that life has a meaning, to fighting for
order and for unity.

Thomas A. Edison

When a man is dead he is dead! My mind is incapable of conceiving
such a thing as a soul. I may be in error, and man may have a
soul; but I simply don't believe it.

Seneca

My ill-health had allowed me a long furlough, when suddenly it
resumed the attack. . . . I do not know why I should call [my ailment]
by its Greek name [asthma]; for it is well enough described as "shortness
of breath." Its attack is of very brief duration, like that of a squall
at sea; it usually ends within an hour. Who indeed could breathe

his last for long? I have passed through all the ills and dangers of the flesh; but nothing seems to me more troublesome than this. And naturally so; for anything else may be called illness; but this is a sort of continued "last gasp." Hence physicians call it "practicing how to die." For some day the breath will succeed in doing what it has so often essayed. Do you think I am writing this letter in a merry spirit, just because I have escaped? It would be absurd to take delight in such supposed restoration to health, as it would be for a defendant to imagine that he had won his case when he had succeeded in postponing his trial. Yet in the midst of my difficult breathing I never ceased to rest secure in cheerful and brave thoughts.

"What?" I say to myself, "Does death so often test me? Let it do so; I myself have for a long time tested death." "When?" you ask. Before I was born. Death is nonexistence, and I know already what that means. What was before me will happen again after me. If there is any suffering in this state, there must have been such suffering also in the past, before we entered the light of day. As a matter of fact, however, we felt no discomfort then. And I ask you, would you not say that one was the greatest of fools who believed that a lamp was worse off when it was extinguished than before it was lighted? We mortals also are lighted and extinguished; the period of suffering comes in between, but on either side there is a deep peace. . . .

He that would not die ought not to live, since death is the condition of life.

Jack London

"I would rather be ashes than dust!" Jack often announced during those last years, and when asked to explain what he meant he would gladly enlarge on the theme: "I would rather that my spark should burn out in a brilliant blaze than it should be stifled by dry-rot. I would rather be a superb meteor, every atom of me in magnificent glow, than a sleepy and permanent planet. The proper function of man is to live, not to exist. I shall not waste my days in trying to prolong them. I shall use my time."

Epicurus

. . . You should accustom yourself to believing that death means
nothing to us, since every good and every evil lies in sensation; but
death is the privation of sensation. Hence a correct comprehension
of the fact that death means nothing to us makes the mortal aspect
of life pleasurable, not by conferring on us a boundless period of
time but by removing the yearning for deathlessness. There is nothing
fearful in living for the person who has really laid hold of the fact
that there is nothing fearful in not living.

PART III

Emotion and Aesthetics

Emotion and Aesthetics

If aesthetics is concerned for the beautiful, it is impossible to separate aesthetics from human emotions. When we say that we were "uplifted," "inspired," or "moved," we refer to feelings at a particular moment in our lives. Peak experiences, which often deal with the beautiful, are emotional experiences.

There was a time, roughly between World Wars I and II, when Humanists treated human beings as one-dimensional entities. Humanism was totally absorbed in rationality, the intellect, the development of the mind. It was even held by some that emotion had no place in Humanism, for emotion was the product of blind faith and supernaturalistic spirituality. Contemporary Humanists, while still holding high the torch of reason, recognize the importance of emotion and of aesthetics in nourishing healthy human beings. Endless disputation and debunking, along with cold, analytical humorless philosophizing, may give employment to pedants in ivy-covered halls but it contributes next to nothing to Humanism as a viable philosophy of living. Without joie de vivre, *Humanism remains a dusty volume on philosophy's shelf in the library of idle speculation. Humanism demands active involvement by individuals in the here and now. How does one achieve* joie de vivre *without an aesthetic sense, without emotion in the conduct of one's life?*

Humanism has yet to develop arts that are uniquely Humanist. Often we have used music from classical composers—or even hymnists—and substituted lyrics more palatable to Humanist thought. We have done this out of desperation, recognizing the void in Humanist aesthetics. The "new wine in old bottles" approach is better than nothing, but it is far from ideal. The challenge to create a Humanist aesthetics remains.

Very few Humanists today continue to embrace the old notion that reason and emotion are antithetical. Instead, most Humanists see reason and emotion as two sides of the same coin, the whole human person. There have been timid beginnings with some innovative creations in audiovisual presentations to fill the immense void in Humanist aesthetics, but there remains an enormous opportunity for musicians, dancers, and artists, in many media.

Love

Erich Fromm

What matters in relation to love is the faith in one's own love; in its ability to produce love in others, and in its reliability.

Robert Green Ingersoll

Love is the only bow on Life's dark cloud. It is the morning and the evening star. It shines upon the babe, and sheds its radiance on the quiet tomb. It is the mother of art, inspirer of poet, patriot and philosopher. It is the air and light of every heart—builder of every home, kindler of every fire on every hearth. It was the first to dream of immortality. It fills the world with melody—for music is the voice of love. Love is the magician, the enchanter, that changes worthless things to joy, and makes right royal kings and queens of common clay. It is the perfume of that wondrous flower, the heart, and without that sacred passion, that divine swoon, we are less than beasts; but with it, earth is heaven, and we are Gods.

Roger E. Greeley

Love Is the Fire That Warms Without a Flame

Love is the fire that warms without a flame.
Love is the fire that never dies.
Love believes in beginning again.
Love is holding on but it is also reaching out (and letting go).
Love steps over disappointment and carries on.
With equal grace love gives and receives a compliment.
Love is ecstasy in the presence of beauty.
Love is the reason we forgive and are forgiven.
Love is passionate dedication to the ideal.
True love is not diminished by misfortune but strengthened.
Love is not ownership or absolute possession but sharing mutuality.
Love is the second mile.
Love keeps our belief in the stars even though we be blind.
Love is the desire to plant trees even though we know that we shall
     never sit in their shade.
Love is not blind but all seeing.
Love does not live because of what we are able to overlook
     but because of what we are able to understand.
Love gives not because it gets but because in the act of giving
     the giver becomes.
When you love something you invest in it because you believe
     that in its realization is a part of your own.
Love is the fire that warms without a flame.
Love is the fire that never dies.

Rupert Brooke

The Great Lover

I have been so great a lover: filled my days
So proudly with the splendor of Love's praise,
The pain, the calm, and the astonishment,
Desire illimitable, and still content,
And all dear names men use, to cheat despair,
For the perplexed and viewless streams that bear
Our hearts at random down the dark of life.
Now, ere the unthinking silence on that strife
Steals down, I would cheat drowsy Death so far,
My night shall be remembered for a star
That outshone all the suns of all men's days.
Shall I not crown them with immortal praise
Whom I have loved, who have given me, dared with me
High secrets, and in darkness knelt to see
The inenarrable godhead of delight?
Love is a flame:—we have beaconed the world's night.
A city:—and we have built it, these and I.
An emperor:—we have taught the world to die.
So, for their sakes I loved, ere I go hence,
And the high cause of Love's magnificence,
And to keep loyalties young, I'll write those names
Golden for ever, eagles, crying flames,
And set them as a banner, that men may know,
To dare the generations, burn and blow
Out on the wind of Time, shining and streaming. . . .

These I have loved:
      White plates and cups, clean-gleaming,
Ringed with blue lines; and feathery, faery dust;
Wet roofs, beneath the lamp-light; the strong crust
Of friendly bread; and many-tasting food;
Rainbows; and the blue bitter smoke of wood;
And radiant raindrops couching in cool flowers;

And flowers themselves, that sway through sunny hours,
Dreaming of moths that drink them under the moon;
Then, the cool kindliness of sheets, that soon
Smooth away trouble; and the rough male kiss
Of blankets; grainy wood; live hair that is
Shining and free; blue-massing clouds, the keen
Unpassioned beauty of a great machine;
The benison of hot water; furs to touch;
The good smell of old clothes; and other such—
The comfortable smell of friendly fingers,
Hair's fragrance, and the musty reek that lingers
About dead leaves and last year's ferns. . . .
　　　　Dear names,
And thousand others throng to me! Royal flames;
Sweet water's dimpling laugh from tap or spring;
Holes in the ground; and voices that do sing;
Voices in laughter, too; and body's pain,
Soon turned to peace; and the deep-panting train;
Firm sands; the little dulling edge of foam
That browns and dwindles as the wave goes home;
And washen stones, gay for an hour; the cold
Graveness of iron; moist black earthen mold;
Sleep; and high places; footprints in the dew;
And oaks; and brown horse-chestnuts, glossy-new;
And new-peeled sticks; and shining pools on grass;—
All these have been my loves. And these shall pass,
Whatever passes not, in the great hour,
Nor all my passion, all my prayers, have power
To hold them with me through the gate of Death.
They'll play deserter, turn with the traitor breath,
Break the high bond we made, and sell Love's trust
And sacramented covenant to the dust.
—Oh, never a doubt but, somewhere, I shall wake,
And give what's left of love again, and make
New friends, now strangers. . . .
　　　　But the best I've known
Stays here, and changes, breaks, grows old, is blown
About the winds of the world, and fades from brains

Of living men, and dies.
      Nothing remains.

O dear my loves, O faithless, once again
This one last gift I give: that after men
Shall know, and later lovers, far-removed,
Praise you, "All these were lovely"; say, "He loved."

Living

Robert Browning

Oh, the wild joys of living! the leaping from rock up to rock,
The strong rending of boughs from the fir-tree, the cool silver shock
Of the plunge in the pool's living water, the hunt of the bear,
And the sultriness showing the lion is couched in his lair.
And the meal, the rich dates yellowed over the gold dust divine,
And the locust-flesh steeped in the pitcher, the full draft of wine,
And the sleep in the dried river-channel where bulrushes tell
That the water was wont to go warbling so softly and well.
How good is man's life, the mere living! how fit to employ
All the heart and the soul and the senses forever in joy!

Joy and Laughter

Robert Green Ingersoll

Laughing has always been considered by theologians as a crime. Ministers have always said you will have no respect for our ideas unless you are solemn. Solemnity is a condition precedent to believing anything without evidence. And if you can only get a man solemn enough, awed enough, he will believe anything.

Why should we postpone our joy to another world? Thousands of people take great pleasure in dancing, and I say, let them dance. Dancing is better than weeping and wailing over a theology born of ignorance and superstition. And so with games of chance. There is a certain pleasure in playing games, and the pleasure is of the most innocent character. Let all these games be played at home and the children will not prefer the saloon to the society of their parents. I believe in cards and billiards. No one should fail to pick up every jewel of joy that can be found in his path. Every person should be as happy as he can provided he is not happy at the expense of another. Let us get all we can of the good between the cradle and the grave, all that we can of the truly dramatic, all that we can of enjoyment. If, when death comes, that is the end, we have at least made the best of this life. If there be another life, let us make the best of that.

Laughter is the blessed boundary line between brute and man. All blessings on the man who first gave the common air the music of laughter—the music that for the moment drove fears from the heart, tears from the eyes, and dimpled cheeks with joy.

In the vase of joy we find some tears.

Joy is wealth and love is the legal tender of the soul.

Hope

Sherwin Wine

Peace needs hope. If we are too impatient with the performance of others, if we expect people to change too quickly, we will despair before we need to.

Utopian fantasies are dangerous. A world in which all hatred and jealousy vanish is not likely. A society in which the danger of war disappears is improbable. A revolution that will abolish all human hostility is a foolish dream. If we expect the impossible, then we will always live with disappointment.

But some dreams are not foolish. They depend for their fulfillment on a patient realism. Armies can be made smaller. Weapons can be reduced in number. Disputes can be resolved through talking. It is possible to make war less warlike and peace more peaceful.

Hope needs perspective and the willingness to settle for undramatic victories. We need to climb our steps one by one.

Erich Fromm

. . . Man is stronger the more fully he is in touch with reality. As long as he is only [a] sheep and his reality is essentially nothing but the fiction built up by his society for more convenient manipulation of men and things, he is weak as a man. . . . Man qua man has an inherent tendency to enlarge his knowledge of reality and that means to approximate the truth. We are not dealing here with a metaphysical concept of truth but with a concept of increasing approximation, which means decreasing fiction and delusion. In comparison with the importance of this increase or decrease of one's grasp of reality, the question whether there is a final truth about anything remains entirely abstract and irrelevant. The process of increasing awareness is nothing but the process of awakening, of opening one's eyes and seeing what is in front of one. Awareness means doing away with illusions and, to the degree that this is accomplished, it is a process of liberation.

Acknowledging Our Emotionality

Sherwin Wine

The risk of being human is always real. To be human is to feel all the feelings the heart can provide. To be human is to hope all the hopes the mind can imagine. We are more than love and kindness. We are more than goodness and tender care. We are also hate and anger. We are also contempt and envy.

Many of us are ashamed to hate, or to be angry, or to feel contempt, or to be jealous. Since we are human and cannot avoid feeling what we feel, since we are human and cannot escape our natural emotions, we deny what we feel. We spend our time refusing what has no need to be refused. We give our precious hours to defending what has no need to be defended. We feel compelled to prove to ourselves and to others that only love fills our hearts and that we seek only to help and never to harm. We are running away from the fullness of our being.

There are moments in life when it is all right to hate, it is good to be angry, it is appropriate to feel contempt. To love all the time is less than human.

PART IV

Ethics

Ethics

Ethics, or morals, are the specific rules or values by which we govern our daily behavior. For the theist, all ethics ultimately are ordained and grounded in "God." There is no way for the devout theist to separate ethics from a deity.

The Humanist believes that it is entirely possible (and desirable) to have ethics independent of a concept of deity. All Humanist ethics are created through the activity of our senses and formulated through the power of reason. Humanists cannot accept the proposition that something is either wrong or right because "God," the Bible, or Jesus so decreed. When Robert Ingersoll was asked to comment on the validity of the biblical commandment "Thou shalt not kill," he replied: "Thou shalt not kill is as old as life itself. And for this reason a large majority of people in all countries have objected to being murdered!" This is a perfectly naturalistic explanation that requires no supernatural sanctions. Humanism recognizes that it is futile to endeavor to codify for all individuals for all time simple dictums governing human behavior.

A simple illustration should suffice. The commandment "Thou shalt not bear false witness" is held by many to be a universal truth, always applicable. I submit that were you a Norwegian child in 1940 and a Nazi soldier asked you, "Do your parents own any guns?" and you were to tell the truth (assuming they did own firearms) you would, in effect, be signing your parents' death warrant if you said "yes." This is but one example. The reader can think of many others. Exceptions to the rule do not, of course, render it worthless. What renders it worthless is to maintain that there can be no exceptions. Ethics demand constant reexamination in the light of our growing knowledge about human beings and the world in which we live.

Ethics can also vary, depending on other ethics held by the individual. Smoking, for example, was declared to be unethical by some people long before the medical verdict was in. It was held that smoking was a waste of time, a foolish expenditure of money, and a nuisance to others in a closed room or car. Whether you happen to agree with this or not, do you not accept that for some people it is a logical, ethical position? Often ethics and rules of conduct produce disagreement and conflict between Humanists. This signifies the importance of understanding ethics, both each other's and the on-going search for new and better ethics. When we argue about ethics we touch the very values upon which we hope to govern our individual lives. What is more important than this? It has been said: "Ethical living is the only reality that gives meaning to religious belief." It can be added that ethical living is the acid test of a Humanist philosophy. If Humanism does not transform the heart and direct one's living, it fails, no matter what other accomplishments it may claim for itself.

Freedom

Sherwin Wine

Every human life is a problem. It is the problem of decision and responsibility. To be human is to be aware of our freedom: our freedom to succeed and our freedom to fail, our freedom to be happy and our freedom to suffer. Many of us do not really want to be free, do not really want to face up to our power. We prefer to plead our weakness and our helplessness. We prefer to blame the fates or destiny, to see the rulers of our lives in the genes of our cells or in the conditioning of our society.

Many people choose to live without dignity. They choose to be like little children and to place the responsibility for their lives in the hands of outside powers. If they are happy it is not because of their decision. And, if they suffer, it is not because of their desire. They are blameless and powerless before the might of the world.

Men and women of dignity are people who see their freedom and value it. They perceive that the quality of their life is their decision and that no suffering justifies passive acceptance. Although they are limited by the human condition, although they are assaulted by natural provocation, they refuse to surrender their self-esteem. For what else is human dignity than to acknowledge that we are masters of our fate and captains of our soul?

Bertrand Russell

The conviction that it is important to believe this or that, even if a free inquiry would not support the belief, is one which is common to almost all religions and which inspires all systems of state education. The consequence is that the minds of the young are stunted and are filled with fanatical hostility both to those who have other fanaticisms and, even more virulently, to those who object to all fanaticisms. . . . The world needs open hearts and open minds, and it is not through rigid systems, whether old or new, that these can be derived.

Albert Camus

What, then, should be the attitude of the rebel? He cannot turn away from the world and from history without denying the very principle of his rebellion, nor can he choose eternal life without resigning himself, in one sense, to evil. If, for example, he is not a Christian, he should go to the bitter end. But to the bitter end means to choose history absolutely and with it murder, if murder is essential to history: to accept the justification of murder is again to deny his origins. If the rebel makes no choice, he chooses the silence and slavery of others. If, in a moment of despair, he declares that he opts both against God and against history, he is the witness of pure freedom; in other words, of nothing. In our period of history and in the impossible condition in which he finds himself, of being unable to affirm a superior motive that does not have its limits in evil, his apparent dilemma is silence or murder—in either case, a surrender.

And it is the same again with justice and freedom. These two demands are already to be found at the beginning of the movement of rebellion and are to be found again in the first impetus of revolution. The history of revolutions demonstrates, however, that they almost always conflict as though their mutual demands were irreconcilable. Absolute freedom is the right of the strongest to dominate. Therefore it prolongs the conflicts that profit by injustice. Absolute justice is achieved by the suppression of all contradiction: therefore it destroys freedom. The revolution to achieve justice, through freedom, ends by aligning them against each other. Thus there exists in every revolution, once the class that dominated up to then has been liquidated, a stage in which it gives birth, itself, to a movement of rebellion which indicates its limits and announces its chances of failure. The revolution, first of all, proposes to satisfy the spirit of rebellion which has given rise to it; then it is compelled to deny it, the better to affirm itself. There is, it would seem, an ineradicable opposition between the movement of rebellion and the attainments of revolution.

. . . . Absolute freedom mocks at justice. Absolute justice denies freedom. To be fruitful, the two ideas must find their limits in each other. No man considers that his condition is free if it is not at the same time just, nor just unless it is free. Freedom, precisely, cannot even be imagined without the power of saying clearly what is just and what is unjust, of claiming all existence in the name of a small part of existence which refuses to die. Finally there is a justice, though a very different kind of justice, in restoring freedom, which is the only imperishable value of history. Men are never really willing to die except for the sake of freedom: therefore they do not believe in dying completely.

Phyllis McGinley

> Ah, snug lie those that slumber
>   Beneath Conviction's roof.
> Their floors are sturdy lumber,
>   Their windows, weatherproof.
> But I sleep cold forever
>   And cold sleep all my kind,
> Both nakedly to shiver
>   In the draft from an open mind.

Robert Green Ingersoll

True religion must be free. Without perfect liberty of mind there can be no true religion. Without liberty the brain is a dungeon—the mind a convict.

Nothing can be more infamous than intellectual tyranny. To put chains upon the body is nothing compared with putting shackles on the brain. No god is entitled to the worship or respect of man who does not give, give to the meanest of his children, every right he claims for himself. If the Pentateuch is true, religious persecution is a duty. The dungeons of the Inquisition were temples and the clank of every chain upon the limbs of heresy was music to the ear of God.

Intellectual liberty is the air of the soul, the sunshine of the mind, and without it, the world is a prison; the universe is a dungeon.

A Christian who does not believe in absolute intellectual liberty is a curse to mankind. An Infidel who does believe in absolute intellectual liberty is a blessing to this world. We cannot expect all infidels to be good, nor all Christians bad, and we might make some mistakes even if we selected these people ourselves. I never did pretend that the fact that a man was a Christian ever tended to show that he was a bad man. Neither have I insisted that the fact that a man is an Infidel even tends to show what, in other respects, his character is.

I have made up my mind that no necessity of bread, or roof, or raiment shall ever put a padlock on my lips. I have made up my mind that no hope of preferment, no honor, no wealth, shall ever make me for one moment swerve from what I really believe, no matter whether it is to my immediate interest, as one would think or not. And while I live, I am going to do what little I can to help my fellow men who have not been as fortunate as I have been. I shall talk on their side. I shall vote on their side.

Ethics

Jacob Bronowski

A rational and coherent system of ethics must grow out of the exploration of the relations between man and society. It will not be a permanent system; it will not teach us what ought to be forever, any more than science teaches us what is forever. Both science and ethics are activities in which we explore relations which, though permanent in the larger sense, are also in constant evolution. This is the nature of the relations of man and society, that they must rest on what is permanently human and yet even this slowly changes and evolves. It is not man and society as they are now that we study, but all the potential which they carry within them by virtue of being human. The studies of a new rationalism are the potential of man in society, and society in man: most deeply, the fulfillment of man.

Gilbert Murray

The whole supposition that a system of violent and intense rewards and punishments is necessary to induce human beings to perform acts for the good of others is based on a false psychology which starts from the individual isolated man instead of man the social animal. Man is an integral member of his group. Among his natural instincts there are those which aim at group-preservation as well as self-preservation; at the good of *autrui* as well as of *moi*. Even among the animals, a cow, a tigress, a hen pheasant, does not need a promise of future rewards to induce her to risk her life to save her young

91

from harm. The male bison or gorilla needs no reward before fighting devotedly for his females and children. They all instinctively care for *autrui*. And it would be a mistake to imagine that this devotion only shows itself in the form of fighting, or only in dangerous crises. It is part of the daily life of any natural group or herd: the strong members help the weak, the weak run for protection to the strong. In man even in his primitive state these instincts are much more highly developed than in the gregarious animals; with the process of civilization they increase in range, in reasonableness, in sublimity. In the late war, how many thousands of men—not particularly selected or high-minded men—risked their lives eagerly to save a companion wounded in No Man's Land? They did not ask or know why they did it. Some may have alleged motives of religion, or motives of ambition in the form of medals or promotions. But the basic motive was probably more or less the same all through; that instinctively they could not see a mate lying there wounded and not try to help him.

John Dewey

Moral goods and ends exist only when something has to be done. The fact that something has to be done proves that there are deficiencies, evils in the existent situation. This ill is just the specific ill that it is. It never is an exact duplicate of anything else. Consequently the good of the situation has to be discovered, projected, and attained on the basis of the exact defect and trouble to be rectified. It cannot intelligently be injected into the situation from without. Yet it is the part of wisdom to compare different cases, to gather together the ills from which humanity suffers, and to generalize the corresponding goods into classes. Health, wealth, industry, temperance, amiability, courtesy, learning, esthetic capacity, initiative, courage, patience, enterprise, thoroughness, and a multitude of other generalized ends are acknowledged as goods. But the *value* of this systematization is intellectual or analytic. Classifications *suggest* possible traits to be on the lookout for in studying a particular case; they suggest methods of action to be tried in removing the inferred causes of ill. They are tools of insight; their value is in promoting an individualized response in the individual situation.

Morals is not a catalogue of acts nor a set of rules to be applied like drugstore prescriptions or cook-book recipes. The need in morals is for specific methods of inquiry to locate difficulties and evils; methods of contrivance to form plans to be used as working hypotheses in dealing with them. And the pragmatic import of the logic of individualized situations, each having its own irreplaceable good and principle, is to transfer the attention of theory from preoccupations with general conceptions to the problem of developing effective methods of inquiry.

Hence, inquiry is exacted; observation of the detailed make-up of the situation; analysis into its diverse factors; clarification of what is obscure; discounting of the more insistent and vivid traits; tracing the consequences of the various modes of action that suggest themselves; regarding the decision reached as hypothetical and tentative until the anticipated or supposed consequences which led to its adoption have been squared with actual consequences. This inquiry is intelligence. Our moral failures go back to some weakness of disposition, some absence of sympathy, some one-sided bias that makes us perform the judgment of the concrete case carelessly or perversely. Wide sympathy, keen sensitiveness, persistence in the face of the disagreeable, balance of interests enabling us to undertake the work of analysis intelligently are the distinctively moral traits—the virtues or moral excellences.

Walter Lippmann

Insofar as men have now lost their belief in a heavenly king, they have to find some other ground for their moral choices than the revelation of his will. It follows necessarily that they must find the tests of righteousness wholly within human experience. The difference between good and evil must be a difference which men themselves recognize and understand. Happiness cannot be the reward of virtue;

it must be the intelligible consequence of it. It follows, too, that virtue cannot be commanded; it must be willed out of personal conviction and desire. Such a morality may properly be called Humanism, for it is centered not in superhuman but in human nature. When men can no longer be theists, they must, if they are civilized, become Humanists. They must live by the premise that whatever is righteous is inherently desirable because experience will demonstrate its desirability. They must live, therefore, in the belief that the duty of man is not to make his will conform to the will of God but to the surest knowledge of the conditions of human happiness.

It is evident that a morality of Humanism presents far greater difficulties than a morality premised on theism. For one thing, it is put immediately to a much severer test. When Kant, for example, argued that theism was necessary to morality, his chief reason was that since the good man is often defeated on earth, he must be permitted to believe in a superhuman power which is "able to connect happiness and morality in exact harmony with each other." Humanism is not provided with such reserves of moral credit; it cannot claim all eternity in which its promises may be fulfilled. Unless its wisdom in any sphere of life is demonstrated within a reasonable time in actual experience, there is nothing to commend it.

A morality of Humanism labors under even greater difficulties. It appears in a complex and changing society; it is an attitude toward life to which rational men necessarily turn whenever their circumstances have rendered a theistic view incredible. It is just because the simpler rules no longer work that the subtler choices of Humanism present themselves. These choices have to be made under conditions, like those which prevail in modern urban societies, where the extreme complexity of rapidly changing human relations makes it very difficult to foresee all the consequences of any moral decision. The men who must make their decisions are skeptical by habit and unsettled amidst the novelties of their surroundings.

The teachers of a theistic morality, when the audience is devout, have only to fortify the impression that the rules of conduct are certified by God the invisible King. The ethical problem for the common man is to recognize the well-known credentials of his teachers. In practice he has merely to decide whether the priest, the prince, and the elders are what they claim to be. When he has done that, there are no radical questions to be asked. But the teachers of Humanism have no credentials. Their teaching is not certified. They have to prove their case by the test of mundane experience. They speak with no authority, which can be scrutinized once and for all, and then forever accepted. They can proclaim no rule of conduct with certainty, for they have no inherent personal authority and they cannot be altogether sure they are right. They cannot command. They cannot truly exhort. They can only inquire, infer, and persuade. They have only human insight to guide them, and those to whom they speak must in the end themselves accept the full responsibility for the consequences of any advice they choose to accept.

Yet with all its difficulties, it is to a morality of Humanism that men must turn when the ancient order of things dissolves. When they find that they no longer believe seriously and deeply that they are governed from heaven, there is anarchy in their souls until by conscious effort they find ways of governing themselves.

Thomas Henry Huxley

The practice of that which is ethically best—what we call goodness or virtue—involves a course of conduct which in all respects is opposed to that which leads to success in the cosmic struggle for existence. In place of ruthless self-assertion it demands self-restraint; in place of thrusting aside, or treading down, all competitors, it requires that the individual shall not merely respect but shall help his fellows. . . . Let us understand once for all, that the ethical progress of society depends not on imitating the cosmic process, still less in running away from it, but in combating it.

Decisiveness and Conviction

Sherwin Wine

Some of us are always waiting. We are waiting for "God" to tell us what to do. We are waiting for destiny to declare our fate. We are waiting for complete understanding before we act out of ignorance. We are waiting for the right mood before we act out of despair. We are waiting for the guarantees of happiness before we dare risk failure. We are even waiting to find ourselves though we are not sure that there is anything to find. We wait and wait and wait. Endless waiting is unattractive. It is a sickness of the will, a disease of the ego. Waiting breeds waiting. As a lifestyle it is more than caution. It is inefficient self-destruction. Postponing decisions is a way of running away from reality. It adds no guarantee, takes away our peace of mind and prevents us from living.

*　　*　　*

If we say that we are intellectual but never read a book; if we say that we are compassionate but never help a neighbor; if we claim to love life but proceed to destroy ourselves, then we are not what we think we are. Behavior always exposes our fantasies. We cannot be what we are unwilling to do.

Watching behavior is the best way to confront reality. It dispels all illusions. It rescues us from phony sincerity. It restores our vision, the only vision that really counts, the vision of truth.

Roger E. Greeley

To make decisions in the light of evidence; to hold fast to the central purpose for our being; to seek solutions to the problems confronting us; to face, together, the facts, no matter how cruel or frustrating; to seek resolutely the realization of self through service to others and ideals; to grow together in fellowship; to go forth in pursuit of the ideal; to hold on to the dream and dispel the nightmare; and above all to be true to the truth and yet remain compassionate: This is our aspiration.

Henri Frederic Amiel

The man who has no refuge in himself, who lives, so to speak, in his front rooms, in the outer whirlwind of things and opinions, is not properly a personality at all; . . . He is one of a crowd, a taxpayer, an elector, an anonymity, but not a man. . . . He who floats with the current, who does not guide himself according to higher principles, who has no ideal, no convictions—such a man is a mere article of the world's furniture—a thing moved, instead of a living and moving being—an echo, not a voice.

Ralph Bunche

Humility toward knowledge, in truth humility in general, is a noble trait. What is more desirable and necessary, in my view, is that one's knowledge be firmly anchored to principle and conviction. In an age in which skepticism, cynicism, and defeatism tend to run rampant, and in which expediency is disturbingly often the dynamic of conduct of individuals and nations alike, there is not only great need for, but great strength to be derived from principle, conviction, and belief.

Be certain always in your minds that you are as right as reason and knowledge can dictate, and then stand by your conclusions and convictions. But keep the door of your minds ever open—avoid the blindness and distortion of unreason, of dogmatism, of prejudice, of demagoguery.

Conscience

Paul Henri Thiry d'Holbach

Our past experiences, the true or false opinions that we form or accept, the rational faculties that we more or less carefully cultivate, the habits that we contract, the education we receive, develop in us an inner feeling of pleasure or pain which we call conscience. This can be defined as the knowledge of the effect our actions produce upon our neighbors and in return upon ourselves.

A little reflection will convince us that, like the instinct or moral sense which we have just spoken of, conscience is an acquired characteristic, and that most moralists have very little foundation for regarding it as an inborn sense, or rather, as a quality inherent in our nature. If we want to agree in the field of ethics, we will be forced to admit that the heart of man is a *tabula rasa,* with a greater or lesser propensity to receive the impressions made upon it.

In the great majority of men, we discern only a faulty conscience, that is, a conscience which judges with little regard for truth or the nature of things, the result of false opinions that we formed or received from others, who succeed in applying the idea of good to actions that would, if closely examined, be considered very harmful. Many people are evil and even commit crimes in all security of conscience, because their consciences are vitiated by prejudice.

There is no vice that does not hide its deformities, when it is approved by the society in which we live; crime itself is glorified by the number and authority of the guilty. No one blushes at adultery or moral turpitude among a corrupt people. No one blushes at being abject as a courtier. The soldier is not ashamed of his plunder and crimes; he even boasts about them to his comrades, for he knows they are ready to do the same. It takes little investigation to find very unjust, mean, inhuman

99

men who do not reproach themselves for their frequent unjust acts, which they often consider legitimate or within their rights, nor for their cruel acts, which they look upon as the results of praiseworthy courage or as duties. We see wealthy people whose consciences are silent about the acquisition of immense fortunes at the expenses of their fellow citizens. Travelers tell us of savages who feel obliged to put their parents to death when decrepitude has rendered them useless. We find zealots whose consciences, blinded by false ideas of virtue, incite them to exterminate remorselessly and without pity all who are not of their opinion. In short, there are nations so vitiated that conscience offers no reproach to men who tolerate plunder, homicide, dueling, adultery, seduction, etc., because these crimes or vices are approved or condoned by public opinion, or are not repressed by law; that being the case, all indulge in them without shame or remorse. These excesses are avoided only by a few who are more moderate, timid and prudent than the rest.

Conscience speaks only to reflective men who rationalize their acts and in whom a respectable education has given rise to an interest and desire to please and an habitual fear of incurring contempt or hatred. A man thus modified becomes capable of self-judgment; he condemns himself when he has committed some deed which he knows may prejudice the feelings he would constantly like to arouse in those whose esteem and love are necessary to his well-being. He experiences shame, remorse and repentance, whenever he does wrong; he examines himself and changes his ways through fear of experiencing again those unhappy feelings which often force him to detest himself, because he sees himself as others see him.

Hence it appears that conscience depends upon an imagination which paints in vivid and unmistakable colors the feelings that we arouse in other people; a man without imagination has little or no sense of these impressions or feelings; he fails to put himself in the place of others. It is very difficult to make a good man of a stupid person, whose imagination tells him nothing, or likewise of a senseless person whose imagination keeps him in a continual state of excitement.

All this proves to us, then, that conscience, far from being a quality inborn or inherent in human nature, can only be the fruit of experience, of imagination guided by reason, the habit of self-examination, the careful supervision of our acts, the foresight to measure their influence on others and their reaction upon ourselves.

Herbert Spencer

To affirm that we know some things to be right and other things to be wrong, by virtue of a supernaturally given conscience; and thus tacitly to affirm that we do not otherwise know right from wrong, is tacitly to deny any natural relations between acts and results. For, if there exist any such relations, then we may ascertain by induction, or deduction, or both, what these are. And if it be admitted that because of such natural relations, happiness is produced by this kind of conduct, which is therefore to be approved, while misery is produced by that kind of conduct, which is therefore to be condemned; then it is admitted that the rightness or wrongness of actions are determined and must finally be determined, by the goodness or badness of the effects that flow from them; which is contrary to the hypothesis.

Ethical Compromise

Sherwin Wine

Peace needs compromise. It needs a willingness to tolerate a world that is less perfect than we want. If we insist on having our way all the time we shall make fighting inevitable.

For some people life is all or nothing. Justice is getting what you deserve, and integrity is never settling for less than you dream of.

For others life is give and take, a balancing act of not so good and not too bad, in endless negotiation among incompatible needs and desires.

People who want the world perfect make revolutions and wars. Peaceful people settle for less—and guarantee the future.

Ethical Behavior

Sherwin Wine

Honesty begins with behavior. What we really think and feel is reflected in what we do. Too often we imagine that we know what we want and believe. We check our conscious mind and encounter numberless ideas and convictions which claim to be the essence of our being. But they are obvious frauds. Our tongue speaks love but our hands speak hate. Our mouth exudes serenity, but our eyes exude fear. Our lips utter friendship, but our whole body screams anger. We feel sincere and so we imagine that we are sincere. We feel honest, and so we imagine that we are honest.

If we listen to our hearts we shall never discover the truth. It is only when we coldly watch our own behavior that we confront reality. Our deepest convictions about ourselves and others can never really be hidden. They boldly proclaim themselves through our actions. While our mouths spin tales of fantasy, our bodies speak with honesty. When we plead that we cannot act on our beliefs we are self-deceived. We always act on what we believe. When we run away from what we say we love, then our love is an illusion. And when we passionately embrace what we say we hate, then our hatred is unreal. We simply are what we do.

Affirmations of Humanism

Paul Kurtz

We are committed to the application of reason and science to the understanding of the universe and to the solving of human problems.

We deplore efforts to denigrate human intelligence, to seek to explain the world in supernatural terms, and to look outside nature for salvation.

We believe that scientific discovery and technology, if used wisely, can contribute immeasurably to the betterment of human life on this planet.

We believe that an open and pluralistic society assures freedom and opportunity for the gretest number of people and that democracy is the best guarantee for protecting human rights from authoritarian elites and repressive majorities.

We are committed to the principle of the separation of church and state and actively resist efforts to impose dogma or ideology by political power.

We cultivate the arts of negotiation and compromise as a means of resolving differences and achieving mutual understanding. The resort to force and violence is anti-humanistic.

We focus on what we can do to make the world a better place in which to live. We are concerned with securing justice and fairness in society and with eliminating discrimination and intolerance.

We believe in supporting the disadvantaged and the handicapped so that they will better be able to help themselves.

We attempt to transcend divisve parochial loyalties based on race, religion, nationality, creed, class, or ethnicity, and strive to work together for the common good of humanity. Although we appreciate the rich diversity of nations and cultures, we recognize that we are all part of the world community.

We are captivated by the beauty of nature. We want to protect and enhance the earth, to preserve it for future generations, and to avoid inflicting needless suffering on other species.

We believe in enjoying life here and now and in developing our creative talents to their fullest. We also believe that living the good life means developing moderation, temperance, and the ability to prudently balance our needs, desires, commitments, and values.

We believe in the cultivation of moral excellence. It is our conviction that it is possible to achieve a joyous and happy life for ourselves and our fellow human beings and to improve the conditions of human life for the benefit of all.

We respect the right to privacy. Mature adults should be allowed to fulfill their aspirations, to express their sexual preferences, to exercise reproductive freedom, to have access to comprehensive and informed healthcare, and to die with dignity—in short, to live as free persons, so long as they do not infringe on the rights of others.

We believe in the common moral decencies: Altruism, integrity, honesty, truthfulness, responsibility. Humanist ethics is amenable to critical, rational guidance. There are normative standards that we discover in working and living together. Moral principles and values are not God-given but are tested by their consequences in human life.

We are deeply concerned with the moral education of our children. We want them to be wholesome, loving, and responsible human beings. We want them to reach their highest potential as individuals, to make wise judgments, to have control over their lives, to function as productive citizens in society, to expand their horizons of learning, and to be sensitive to needs of others. We want to nourish their ability to reason and be compassionate.

We are engaged by the arts no less than by the sciences. Poetry, music, drama, and the fine arts are a source of heightened awareness and significant enrichment.

We are citizens of the universe, impressed by the great adventures in modern science. As we probe into the nature of subatomic particles, evolving life forms, and distant galaxies, we are excited by the possibilites of discoveries still to be made in the cosmos.

We are skeptical of untested claims to knowledge, but we are open to novel ideas and seek new departures in our thinking.

We affirm Humanism as a realistic alternative to theologies of despair and ideologies of violence. This life need not be a tragic vale of tears devoid of meaning and hope. Humanism is a source of rich personal significance and of genuine satisfaction in service to others. Humanism is progressive, adventurous, outgoing, creative, and exuberant.

We believe in optimism rather than pessimism, hope rather than despair, learning in the place of dogma, truth instead of ignorance, joy rather than guilt or sin, tolerance in the place of fear, love instead of hatred, compassion over selfishness, beauty instead of ugliness, and reason rather than blind faith or irrationality.

As Humanists we believe in the fullest realization of the best and noblest that we are capable of as human beings.

PART V

Happiness

Happiness

"While I am opposed to all orthodox creeds, I have a creed of my own and my creed is this:

> *Reason is the only torch,*
> *Justice the only worship,*
> *Humanity the only religion,*
> *Love the only priest,*
> *Happiness the only good.*

The time to be happy is now. The place to be happy is here. The way to be happy is to help make others so." So said Robert Green Ingersoll.

More than one hundred years have passed since Ingersoll offered his "personal creed" in response to orthodox criticism that "one must have a creed by which to live." While we can fault it today for its lack of attention to the relationship of the human species to all else that lives, as a general admonition it stands. It is not likely, as some have said, that we will ignore our own needs if we take seriously the last sentence in Ingersoll's creed. I think that we can safely run that risk without jeopardizing our well-being.

Humanism has had many critics. Not all the criticisms levied have been off the mark, that is, irresponsible smears by "hate-mongers." Not at all. Let us admit that within the fold of Humanists, hedonism has raised its head, here and there, now and then. Hedonism is sometimes confused with happiness and thus has been embraced by some Humanists. It is a case of overreaction. When some took off the Puritanical hairshirt, they decided that henceforth their sole concern in life would be satisfying their every whim and appetite— regardless of its impact on others. The result of this kind of behavior is tragic and unethical. If we would become human, we cannot do it alone or by disregarding the rights, needs, and happiness of others. ("In others' nobility we chiefly find our own!")

Happy people are able to laugh at their own absurd predicament, their foibles and failures, minor tragedies and errors. Above and beyond their own circumstances, they enjoy a good laugh at their own and others' expense, for is not humor predicated on some misfortune, lack, or distortion in oneself or another? Happy people enjoy a good story, share it with others, and thus bring them happiness.

Humanism must not be humorless, though many Humanists whose works are printed appear to be just that. Does not happiness generally depend on how you relate to yourself, to others, and to your work? For Humanists in particular, however, happiness also depends on whether we have accepted the reality of our mortality and decided that life is nevertheless worth living. This is no easy task, and yet it is the first step for those who would be happy Humanists. It is perhaps the most difficult step to take, but it is imperative for those who want to live a life that is, in essence, truly self-motivated and inner-directed, and one that is not based on some reward and punishment mechanism said to become operative in the "next life."

If you would be happy, align yourself with happy people, worthwhile endeavors, creative efforts, and seek to be useful to those whose lives you touch.

Here and Now

Anonymous

I shall pass through this world but once. Any good therefore that I can do, or any kindness that I can show to any human being, let me do it now. Let me not defer it or neglect it, for I shall not pass this way again.

Happiness

Sherwin Wine

We live and find it hard to live. We are consumed by anxiety and we know that nature is stingy with satisfaction. We are terrified by the limits of our wisdom and we shiver in the cold of human ignorance. Love touches us with the pleasure of fulfillment and runs away too soon. Pain squeezes the marrow of our bones and lingers with malice. Although our suffering cries out for justice, the world answers with deaf defiance. The darkness of evil is a persistent shadow.

We live and find it good to live. We feel the invitation of doing and we rush to the surprise of new excitement. We see the opportunity of our talents and we plunge to taste their fulfillment. Bold events stimulate our senses and tease the ordering skill of our reason. Unselfish acts overwhelm our fears and fill our hearts with the security of love. The world is an open door to vital variety and stuns our hopes with boundless promise. The light of our possibility shines through to overwhelm the darkness.

Robert Green Ingersoll

Any man who believes that he can make some God happy by making himself miserable is superstitious. Anyone who believes he can gain happiness in another world by raising hell with his fellowman in this, is simply superstitious. . . . He who believes that there is, or that there can be any other religious duty than to increase the happiness of mankind in the world now and here, is simply superstitious.

112

Bertrand Russell

Certain things are indispensable to the happiness of most men, but these are simple things: food and shelter, health, love, successful work and the respect of one's own herd. To some people parenthood also is essential. Where these things are lacking, only the exceptional man can achieve happiness; but where they are enjoyed, or can be obtained by well-directed effort, the man who is still unhappy is suffering from some psychological maladjustment. . . .

It should be our endeavor . . . to aim at avoiding self-centered passions and at acquiring those affections and those interests which will prevent our thoughts from dwelling perpetually upon ourselves. It is not the nature of most men to be happy in a prison, and the passions which shut us up in ourselves constitute one of the worst kinds of prisons. Among such passions some of the commonest are fear, envy, the sense of sin, self-pity and self-admiration. In all these our desires are centered upon ourselves: there is no genuine interest in the outer world, but only a concern lest it should in some way injure us or fail to feed our ego. . . .

The happy life is to an extraordinary extent the same as the good life. Professional moralists have made too much of self-denial, and in so doing have put the emphasis in the wrong place. Conscious self-denial leaves a man self-absorbed, and vividly aware of what he has sacrificed. . . . What is needed is not self-denial, but that kind of direction of interest outward which will lead spontaneously and naturally to the same acts that a person absorbed in the pursuit of his own virtue could only perform by means of conscious self-denial. . . .

There is another difference, somewhat more subtle, between the attitude towards life that I have been recommending and that which is recommended by the traditional moralists. The traditional moralist, for example, will say that love should be unselfish. In a certain sense he is right, that is to say, it should not be selfish beyond a point, but it should undoubtedly be of such a nature that one's own happiness is bound up in its success. If a man were to invite a lady to marry him on the ground that he ardently desired her happiness and at the same time considered that she would afford him ideal opportunities of self-abnegation, I think it may be doubted whether she would be altogether pleased. Undoubtedly we should desire the happiness of those whom we love, but not as an alternative to our own. In fact the whole antithesis between self and the rest of the world, which is implied in the doctrine of self-denial, disappears as soon as we have any genuine interest in persons or things outside ourselves. Through such interests a man comes to feel himself part of the stream of life, not a hard separate entity like a billiard ball, which can have no relation with other such entities except that of collision. . . . The happy man is the man . . . whose personality is neither divided against itself nor pitted against the world. Such a man feels himself a citizen of the universe, enjoying freely the spectacle that it offers, and the joys that it affords, untroubled by the thought of death because he feels himself not really separate from those who will come after him. It is in such profound instinctive union with the stream of life that the greatest joy is to be found.

Anticipation

Clarence Darrow

All my life I have been planning and hoping and thinking and dreaming and loitering and waiting. All my life I have been getting ready to begin to do something worth the while. I have been waiting for the summer and waiting for the fall; I have been waiting for the winter and waiting for the spring; waiting for the night and waiting for the morning; waiting and dawdling and dreaming, until the day is almost spent and the twilight close at hand.

Affirmation of Life

Corliss Lamont

Often it is claimed that those who have given up supernatural religion have nothing positive to offer humanity in place of the old, age-hallowed myths. This is very far indeed from the actual truth. The Humanist conception of life constitutes a profound and passionate affirmation of the joys and beauties, the braveries and idealisms, of existence on this earth. This philosophy, while it provides the most effective of all answers to death, has by no means been motivated primarily by the fact of mortality. It stands on its own feet as an independent and forthright expression of human living at its fullest and best.

The Humanist attitude does not mean merely the happy acceptance and cultivation of the numberless goods of an abundant Nature. It also means that, however desirable a long and rounded life may be, the *quality of life* counts above all. It means that however rich and worthwhile may be the more pleasing human experiences, there may come a time when an individual must forego personal contentment to stand up for the things which he holds dear. It means that however wholesome may be the full-hearted enjoyment of the quickly passing present, there is always our obligation to the future and to the ideal of human progress. Particularly is this true in this extremely exciting but troubled period of world history, when mankind is beset on every side with the most momentous problems.

It remains to be said that no matter how bleak the fortunes of the world may appear at any particular moment, a certain philosophical optimism is always justified. Not only are the potentialities of man in energy and intelligence well-nigh inexhaustible, but life and the affirmation of life will in all probability endure throughout the eternities of time left to this sun-warmed, revolving earth.

PART VI

Human Nature

Human Nature

Are human beings inherently evil as stated in the Catholic doctrine of original sin? Or are they inherently good? Are we born a tabula rasa, *on which experience will write our conduct and character? Surely, no Humanist accepts that all humans are born bad—or inherently good, for that matter. At the same time, the environmental determinists are not without their critics among thoughtful Humanists. Beyond all of these arguments, pro and con, stand the contributions of Sigmund Freud. It was Freud who radically rethought the nature of human nature. Freud's impact on psychology and the traditional biblical view of human nature cannot be overstated. Along with Charles Darwin, Freud revolutionized our view of ourselves. In no way has time eroded his most basic contribution to understanding human nature.*

Freud's contention that early childhood experiences shape adult attitudes and behaviors stands as a fundamental truth. Prior to Freud, the predominant view of human beings swung between foreordained predestination and an ongoing war between good and evil, Satan versus God, the outcome being what determined human behavior. Mental illness was simply the Devil gaining the upper hand in an individual. Just as Darwin demolished "special creation," Freud laid the Devil to rest with his powerful insights into human beings, their basic nature, and how the latter came to be influenced and developed through interaction with parents, siblings, and society at large.

119

Every now and then as we walk by a church's announcement board, we may read a sermon title that states: "The Problem of Evil" or "Good and Evil and God." Apparently Freud has had little influence on the pastors who write such sermons because good and evil are still being treated as forces that enter and leave our persons at will, divinely decreed or directed. Humanists since Freud usually view good and evil as the result of environment and education, while allowing for disturbances that are organic in nature. The more we study the human animal, the more it appears that there may well be genetically predetermined predispositions to such maladies as alcoholism, schizophrenia, and a number of other psychological disorders or diseases. Apart from these observations the most basic Humanist view of human nature is best expressed by the saying, "To be human is not a fact but a task." Humanists may be excessively optimistic in this regard, but what other view of human growth and development has any meaning whatsoever? We must not resign ourselves to any fatalistic determinism, be it theological or psychological.

Soul

Clarence Darrow

Every man knows when his life began; can one imagine an organism that has a beginning and no end? If I did not exist in the past, why should I, or could I, exist in the future? We are told by some that we had no beginning; what evidence exists that this is true? I have no remembrance of the clash of worlds, or the other seeming catastrophes out of which the earth was born. I have no remembrance of the flood. I do not recall Joshua or Caesar or Hannibal or Napoleon or Wellington. I have no remembrance of Anthony or Cleopatra. I cannot remember George Washington or the eight years' war which separated Europe from the United States. I do not remember the French Revolution that shook the political and social world to its foundation. I cannot recall the battle of Waterloo or even the surrender of Cornwallis. I had not then been born and did not exist. I have only read about these people and events.

But how about the happenings of my own life? I have no remembrance of the months that I lay in my mother's womb. I cannot recall the day of my birth or the time when I first opened my eyes to the light of the sun. I cannot remember when I was an infant or when I began to creep on the floor, or when I was taught to walk, or anything before I was five or six years old. Still, all of these were important, wonderful, and strange in a new life. What I call my consciousness, for lack of a better word and a better understanding, came from my growth and the experiences that I met at every turn. I have a hazy recollection of the burial of a soldier who was shot toward the end of the Civil War. He was buried near the schoolhouse when I was seven years old. But I have no remembrance of the assassination of Abraham Lincoln, although

I must then have been eight years old. I must have known about it at the time, as my family and my community idolized Abraham Lincoln, and all America was in mourning at his death. Why do I remember the dead boy soldier who was buried a year before? Perhaps because I knew him well; perhaps because his family was close to my childish life; possibly because it came to me as my first knowledge of death. At all events it made so deep an impression that in a misty way I recall it now. Many of the events of the first ten or twelve years of my life are now entirely forgotten. So far as these events are concerned, the mind and consciousness of the boy [I was] are already dead.

Am I now fully alive? I am seventy-one years old. I often fail to recollect the names of some of those whom I knew full well. Many events do not make the lasting impression that they once did. I know that it will be only a few years, even if my body still survives decay, when few important things will even register in my mind. I know how it is with the old. I know that physical life in a way can persist beyond the time when the brain can fully function. I know that if I live to an extreme old age my mind will fail; that I will eat and drink and go to my bed and to the table in an automatic way. I know that memory, which is all that binds me to the past, will already be dead. I know that all that will remain will be a vegetative existence; that I will sit and doze in the chimney corner, and my body will measurably function even though the ego is already practically dead. I am sure that if I shall die of what is called old age, my consciousness will gradually go with my failing emotions, and that I will no more be aware of the near approach of final dissolution than will the dying tree.

Sin and Evil

Alfred Adler

Those who have not been torn out of their social relationships by the complicated muddle of our educational system are best adapted to pursue researches in human nature. We are dealing with men and women who are, in the last analysis, either optimists, or fighting pessimists who have not been driven to resignation by their pessimism. But contact with humanity, alone, is not enough. There must be experience as well. A real appreciation of human nature, in the face of our inadequate education today, will be gained only by one class of human beings. These are the contrite sinners, either those who have been in the whirlpool of psychic life, entangled in all its mistakes and errors, and saved themselves out of it, or those who have been close to it and felt its currents touching them. Others naturally can learn it, especially when they have the gift of identification, the gift of empathy. The best knower of the human soul will be the one who has lived through human passions himself. The contrite sinner seems as valuable a type in our day and age as he was in the days when the great religions developed. He stands much higher than a thousand righteous ones. How does this happen? An individual who has lifted himself above the difficulties of life, extricated himself from the swamp of living, found power to profit by bad experiences, and elevate himself as a result of them, understands the good and the bad sides of life. No one can compare with him in this understanding, certainly not the righteous one.

Gilbert Murray

All the subtle explanations of modern theology really fail to provide us with a solution of the fundamental and glaring contradiction involved in all religions which maintain that a world, admitted to be full of evil, is created and ordered by the will of a being who is perfectly good and also omnipotent. The hypothesis of an "intractable material" which the good God cannot control is inconsistent with his omnipotence. The hypothesis that he left man's will free to do good or evil as it chose is inconsistent with his perfect goodness, and fails entirely to meet the difficulties presented by a "Nature red in tooth in claw with ravin," in which every creature normally lives by inflicting pain and death on others, and cannot live otherwise. Another hypothesis is that we are mistaken in supposing that there is any evil in the world: all is really just as it ought to be. Either no Jews are persecuted, no Chinese massacred, no men or animals perishing in torture, or, if there are, it is good for them, and if they had sense they would like it. This doctrine is, in its ordinary forms, heartless as well as senseless. It is not only obviously untrue, but like the doctrine of eternal damnation it is an untruth which, in the natural meaning of the words, no feeling man could believe. But there is another sense in which it can be understood and may, as far as logic goes, be true; only in that case it utterly wrecks the current conceptions of theism. It may be that what man calls "good" is not at all the same as what the power behind the world calls "good." That Power may well be no more "good" or "just" or "merciful" than it is "polite" or "clever" or "agreeable" or a "good linguist." All our moral ideas may be as inapplicable to it as our social phrases and conventional prejudices. Such a Power is neither good nor evil, neither friend nor enemy. It cannot be loved or hated. It is not anthropomorphic, not human, not describable in human language—not what we mean by God.

Walter Lippmann

The greatest of all perplexities in theology has been to reconcile the infinite goodness of God with his omnipotence. Nothing puts a greater strain upon the faith of the common man than the existence of utterly irrational suffering in the universe, and the problem which tormented Job still troubles every devout and thoughtful man who beholds the monstrous injustices of nature. If there were no pain in the world except that which was felt by responsible beings who had knowingly transgressed some law of conduct, there would, of course, be no problem of evil. Pain would be nothing but a rational punishment. But the pain which is suffered by those who according to all human standards are innocent, by children and by animals, for example, cannot be fitted into any rational theory of reward and punishment. It never has been. The classic attempts to solve the problem of evil invariably falsify the premises. This falsification may for a time satisfy the inquirer, but it does not settle the problem. That is why the problem is forever presenting itself again. . . .

. . . For things are neutral, and evil is a certain way of experiencing them.

To realize this is to destroy the awfulness of evil. I use the word "awful" in its exact sense, and I mean that in abandoning the notion that evil has to be reconciled with a theory of how the world is governed, we rob it of universal significance. We deflate it. . . . It may be said that the effect of the modern approach is to take evils out of the context of superstition.

They cease to be signs and portents symbolizing the whole of human destiny and become specific and distinguishable situations which have to be dealt with. The effect of this is not only to limit drastically the meaning, and therefore the dreadfulness, of any evil, but to substitute for a general sense of evil an analytical estimate of particular evils. They are then seen to be of long duration and of short, preventable, curable, or inevitable. As long as all evils are believed somehow to fit into a divine, if mysterious, plan, the effort to eradicate them must seem on the whole futile, and even impious. The history of medical progress offers innumerable instances of how men have resisted the introduction of sanitary measures because they dreaded to interfere with the providence of God. It is still felt, I believe, in many quarters, even in medical circles, that to mitigate the labor pains in childbirth is to blaspheme against the commandment that in pain children shall be brought forth. An aura of dread surrounds evil as long as evil situations remain entangled with a theory of divine government.

Individuality

John Stuart Mill

The only part of the conduct of any one, for which he is amenable to society, is that which concerns others. In the part which merely concerns himself, his independence is, of right, absolute. Over himself, over his own body and mind, the individual is sovereign.

Rebellion

Albert Camus

Rebellion is born of the spectacle of irrationality, confronted with an unjust and incomprehensible condition. But its blind impulse is to demand order in the midst of chaos, and unity in the very heart of the ephemeral. It protests, it demands, it insists that the outrage be brought to an end, and that what has up to now been built upon shifting sands should henceforth be founded on rock. . . . Man is the only creature who refuses to be what he is.

Humanity

Sophocles

Wonders are many, and none is more wonderful than man; the power that crosses the white sea, driven by the stormy south-wind, making a path under surges that threaten to engulf him; and Earth, the eldest of the gods, the immortal, the unwearied, doth he wear, turning the soil with the offspring of horses, as the ploughs go to and fro from year to year.

And the light-hearted race of birds, and the tribes of savage beasts, and the sea-brood of the deep, he snares in the meshes of his woven toils, he leads captive, man excellent in wit. And he masters by his arts the beasts whose lair is in the wilds, who roams the hills; he tames the horse of shaggy mane, he puts the yoke upon its neck, he tames the tireless mountain bull.

And speech, and wind-swift thought, and all the moods that mould a state, hath he taught himself; and how to flee the arrows of the frost, when 'tis hard lodging under the clear sky, and the arrows of the rushing rain; yea, he hath resource for all; without resource he meets nothing that must come: only against Death shall he call for aid in vain; but from baffling maladies he hath devised escapes.

129

Creeds and Commandments

Robert Green Ingersoll

I do believe in the nobility of human nature. I believe in love and home, kindness and humanity. I believe in good fellowship and cheerfulness, in making wife and children happy. I believe in good nature, in giving to others all of the rights that you claim for yourself. I believe in free thought, in reason, observation, and experience. I believe in self-reliance and in expressing your honest thought. I have hope for the whole human race. What will happen to one will, I hope, happen to all and that, I hope, will be good. Above all, I believe in liberty . . . I believe in the fireside. I believe in the democracy of home. I believe in the republicanism of the family. I believe in liberty, equality and love.

We are not endeavouring to chain the future, but to free the present. We are not forging fetters for our children, but we are breaking those our fathers made for us. We are the advocates of inquiry, of investigation and thought. This of itself is an admission that we are not perfectly satisfied with all our conclusions. Philosophy has not the egotism of faith. While superstition builds walls and creates obstructions, science opens all the highways of thought. We do not pretend to have circumnavigated everything, and to have solved all difficulties, but we do believe that it is better to love men than to fear gods; that it is grander and nobler to think and investigate for yourself than to repeat a creed. We are satisfied that there can be but little liberty on earth while men worship a tyrant in heaven. We do not expect to accomplish everything in our day; but we want to do what good we can, and to render all the service possible in the holy cause of human progress. We know that doing away with gods and supernatural persons and powers is not an end. It is a means to an end—the real end being the happiness of man. . . .

For thousands of years men have been writing the real Bible, and it is being written from day to day, and it will never be finished while man has life. All the facts that we know, all the truly recorded events, all the discoveries and inventions, all the wonderful machines whose wheels and levers seem to think, all the poems, crystals from the brain, flowers from the heart, all the songs of love and joy, of smiles and tears, the great dramas of Imagination's world, the wondrous paintings, the miracles of form and color, of light and shade, the marvelous marbles that seem to live and breathe, the secrets told by rock and star, by dust and flower, by rain and snow, by frost and flame, by winding stream and desert sand, by mountain range and billowed sea.

All the wisdom that lengthens and ennobles life—all that avoids or cures disease, or conquers pain—all just and perfect laws and rules that guide and shape our lives, all thoughts that feed the flames of love, the music that transfigures, enraptures and enthralls, the victories of heart and brain, the miracles that hands have wrought, the deft and cunning hands of those who worked for wife and child, the histories of noble deeds, of brave and useful men, of faithful, loving wives, of quenchless mother-love, of conflicts for the right, of sufferings for the truth, of all the best that all the men and women of the world have said, and thought and done through all the years.

These treasures of the heart and brain—these are the Sacred Scriptures of the human race.

Sherwin Wine

1. Do not feel absolutely certain of anything.
2. Do not think it worth while to produce belief by concealing evidence, for the evidence is sure to come to light.

3. Never try to discourage thinking, for you are sure to succeed.

4. When you meet with opposition, even if it should come from children, endeavor to overcome it by argument and not by authority, for a victory dependent upon authority is unreal and illusory.

5. Have no respect for the authority of others, for there are always contrary authorities to be found.

6. Do not use power to suppress opinions you think pernicious, for if you do the opinions will suppress you.

7. Do not fear to be eccentric in opinion, for every opinion now accepted was once eccentric.

8. Find more pleasure in intelligent dissent than in passive agreement, for if you value intelligence as you should, the former implies a deeper agreement than the latter.

9. Be scrupulously truthful, even when truth is inconvenient, for it is more inconvenient when you try to conceal it.

10. Do not feel envious of the happiness of those who live in a fool's paradise for only a fool will think that it is happiness.

Courage

Bertrand Russell

We want to stand upon our own feet and look fair and square at the world—its good facts, its bad facts, its beauties, and its ugliness; see the world as it is and be not afraid of it. Conquer the world by intelligence and not merely by being slavishly subdued by the terror that comes from it. The whole conception of God is a conception derived from the ancient Oriental despotisms. It is a conception quite unworthy of free men. We ought to stand up and look the world frankly in the face. We ought to make the best we can of the world and if it is not so good as we wish, after all it will still be better than what these others have made it in all these ages. A good world needs knowledge, kindliness and courage; it does not need a regretful hankering after the past or the fettering of the free intelligence by the words uttered long ago by ignorant men. It needs a fearless outlook and a free intelligence. It needs hope for the future, not looking back all the time toward a past that is dead, which we trust will be far surpassed by the future that our intelligence can create.

William Ernest Henley

Invictus

Out of the night that covers me,
   Black as the Pit from pole to pole,
I thank whatever gods may be
   For my unconquerable soul.

In the fell clutch of circumstance
   I have not winced nor cried aloud.
Under the bludgeonings of chance
   My head is bloody, but unbowed.

Beyond this place of wrath and tears
   Looms but the Horror of the shade,
And yet the menace of the years
   Finds and shall find me unafraid.

It matters not how strait the gate,
   How charged with punishments the scroll,
I am the master of my fate:
   I am the captain of my soul.

PART VII

Naturalism

Naturalism

Responding to a conventional religious spokesman, I once described myself as a "scientific, evolutionary, naturalistic Humanist." Each of the qualifying adjectives is important in taking Humanism out of a narrow philosophy which, near the turn of the century, substituted man for "God" as the object of worship. At that time, man was not only the "measure of all things," but he was also a life-form viewed as being different in kind—and not simply in degree—from all other life-forms. This new kind of "special creation" popularized by Humanists seemed to make man independent, somehow divorced from all other life-forms. This was a tragic error and did nothing to enhance Humanism, particularly after the disclosures of World War II deathcamps. (After Auschwitz, who could ever worship man again?)

Beginning with Ellen Swallow, ecology began to show that homo sapiens *was interdependent with all that lives, that in the chain of life, man was but a single link. These ideas began to influence the direction of Humanist thought. Naturalism became much more than simply the opposite of supernaturalism. It was Julian Huxley who brought biology and ecology into Humanist thought, to which his contributions were enormous. He declared, not long after World War II, which took tens of millions of lives, "Population is the problem of our age!" This view was not widely accepted and almost nowhere was it applauded.*

Keenly aware that man was a natural phenomenon and not a special creation ordained by some remote deity, Huxley urged humanity to assume full responsibility for human destiny. Living as we do in a natural universe, there is no supernatural agency governing human destiny. In partnership with all that lives and supports life, humanity must assume full responsibility for the future of this planet. In this regard, Sir Julian dared to think the unthinkable, dared discuss the forbidden as he championed both euthanasia and eugenics.

Homo sapiens *has no natural predator to control the species numbers. War is not a very humane method by which to regulate population growth. In a natural universe, the unnatural methods of artificial birth control, eugenics, abortion, and euthanasia are imperative measures if the population bomb is to be defused. The excessive optimism of late-19th-century Humanists blinded them to the need for linking humanity's future to all of life and to earth's finite and fragile resources.*

Phrases such as unlimited resources *and* Nature's seemingly inexhaustible storehouse *led Humanists to promote technology and the mass production of goods and services independently of ecological considerations. This was believed to be the way in which to achieve the millennium soon. In the second half of this century, Humanists and others have come to the realization that the species cannot improve or even endure without accepting the laws of the natural world. No matter whether we are the highest life-form or not, we cannot continue to ignore the laws of nature, the ecological considerations of our biosphere. Thus, naturalism is much more than a rejection of supernaturalism. Other aspects of naturalism will be found in the selections that follow.*

The Unknown

Epicurus

It must be admitted that the fundamental disturbance of the human soul springs first of all from men's considering phenomena as caused by human beings to whom they attribute will, action, and motive power; then by the fact that men, believing in myths, will always fear something terrible, everlasting punishment as certain or probable, and are even frightened of the insensibility of death, as if we should be conscious of it; and finally by the fact that, as a result, men base all these fears not on mature opinions, but on irrational fancies, so that they are more disturbed by fear of the unknown than by facing facts. Peace of mind lies in being delivered from all these fears.

Thanksgiving

Robert Green Ingersoll

Whom do I thank? I thank the father who spoke the first gentle word, the mother who first smiled upon her babe. I thank those who built rude homes and watched the faces of their happy children in the glow of fireside flames. . . . I thank the poets of the dawn—the tellers of legends—the makers of myths—the singers of joy and grief, of hope and love. I thank the industrious men, the loving mothers, the useful women. They are the benefactors of our race. I thank the heroes, the destroyers of prejudice and fear—the dethroners of savage gods—the extinguishers of hate's eternal fire—the heroes, the breakers of chains—the founders of free states, the makers of just laws . . . the apostles of reason, the disciples of truth, the soldiers of freedom—the heroes who held high the holy torch and filled the world with light. With all my heart, I thank them all!

Risk

Roger E. Greeley

Rarely are we able to feel comfortable that "we are doing the right thing" when there is a conflict of competing values. We must nevertheless be decisive and willing to run the risk of being wrong but "risking" in such a manner that if we do err, it is an honest mistake and not a display of arbitrary power.

Sophocles

Numberless wonders
terrible wonders walk the world but none the match for man—
that great wonder crossing the heaving gray sea,
driven on by the blasts of winter
on through breakers crashing left and right,
holds his steady course
and the oldest of the gods he wears away—
the Earth, the immortal, the inexhaustible—
as his plows go back and forth, year in, year out
with the breed of stallions turning up the furrows.

And the blithe, lightheaded race of birds he snares,
the tribes of savage beasts, the life that swarms the depths—
with one fling of his nets
woven and coiled tight, he takes them all,
man the skilled, the brilliant!
He conquers all, taming with his techniques
the prey that roams the cliffs and wild lairs,
training the stallion, clamping the yoke across
his shaggy neck, and the tireless mountain bull.

And speech and thought, quick as the wind
and the mood and mind for law that rules the city—
all these he has taught himself
and shelter from the arrows of the frost
when there's rough lodging under the cold clear sky
and the shafts of lashing rain—
ready, resourceful man!
Never without resources
never an impasse as he marches on the future—
only Death, from Death alone he will find no rescue
but from desperate plagues he has plotted his escapes.

Purpose

Albert Einstein

Strange is our situation here on earth. Each of us comes for a short visit, not knowing why, yet sometimes seeming to divine a purpose. From the standpoint of daily life, however, there is one thing we do know: that man is here for the sake of other men—above all for those upon whose smiles and well-being our own happines depends. . . . Many times a day I realize how much of my outer and inner life is built upon the labors of my fellowmen, both living and dead, and how earnestly I must exert myself in order to give as much as I have received.

Roger E. Greeley

A man in quest of a difficult star cannot allow the taint of unbecoming means to prostitute the high resolve that he espouses. Frustration can corrupt the noblest purpose blindly held but the noblest purpose clearly perceived is incorruptible. Blind commitment may blaze but it is tenuous and often self-destructive. Only the clearest view of the end can ennoble and sustain the means.

Henry Miller

To imagine that we are going to be saved by outside intervention, whether in the shape of an analyst, a dictator, a savior, or even God, is sheer folly. There are not enough lifeboats to go around, and anyway . . . what is needed more than lifeboats is lighthouses. A fuller, clearer vision—not more safety appliances.

John Stuart Mill

Questions of ultimate ends are not amenable to direct proof. Whatever can be proved to be good must be so by being shown to be a means to something admitted to be good without proof. . . . The art of music is good, for the reason among others, that it produces pleasure; but what proof is it possible to give that pleasure is good?

Johann Bojer

We are flung by an indifferent law of the universe into a life we cannot order as we would; we are ravaged by injustice, by sickness and sorrow, by fire and flood. In our own home we are but on a visit. And yet man smiles and laughs in the face of his tragic fate; in the midst of his thraldom, he has created the beautiful on earth. In the midst of his torments he has had so much surplus energy of soul that he has sent it radiating forth into the cold depths of space and warmed them with the divine. So marvelous art thou, O spirit of man!

Thou dost reap death, and in return thou sowest the dream of everlasting life. Each of us brought our ray in the mighty sea of light, each of us, from primitive men setting up the first mark above the grave of his dead, to the genius raising the pillars of a temple towards heaven. Honor to thee, O spirit of man! Thou givest a soul to the world, thou settest it a goal; thou art the hymn that lifts it into harmony. Therefore, turn back into thyself, lift high thy head and meet proudly the evil that comes to thee. Though adversity crush thee, though death blot thee out, yet art thou still unconquerable and eternal.

Nature

A. Eustace Haydon

The Humanist rarely loses the feeling of perfect at-homeness in the universe. He is conscious of himself as an earth-child. There is a mystic glow in this sense of belonging. Memories of his long ancestry still linger in muscle and nerve, in brain and germ cell. On moonlit nights, in the renewal of life in the springtime, before the glory of a sunset, in moments of swift insight he feels the community of his own physical being with the body of his mother earth. Rooted in millions of years of planetary history, he has a secure feeling of being at home and a consciousness of pride and dignity as a bearer of the heritage of the ages.

George Gordon, Lord Byron

Where rose the mountains, there to him were friends;
Where roll'd the ocean, thereon was his home;
Where a blue sky, and glowing clime, extends,
He had the passion and the power to roam;
The desert, forest, cavern, breaker's foam,
Were unto him companionship; they spake
A mutual language, clearer than the tome
Of his land's tongue, which he would oft forsake
For Nature's pages glass'd by sunbeams on the lake.

    .   .   .   .   .

I live not in myself, but I become
Portion of that around me; and to me
High mountains are a feeling, but the hum
Of human cities torture: I can see
Nothing to loathe in nature, save to be
A link reluctant in a fleshly chain,
Class'd among creatures, when the soul can flee,
And with the sky, the peak, the heaving plain
Of ocean, or the stars, mingle, and not in vain.

    .   .   .   .   .

Are not the mountains, waves, and skies a part
Of me and of my soul, as I of them?
Is not the joy of these deep in my heart
With a pure passion? should I not contemn
All objects, if compared with these? and stem
A tide of suffering, rather than forego
Such feelings for the hard and worldly phlegm
Of those whose eyes are only turn'd below,
Gazing upon the ground, with thoughts which dare not glow?

    .   .   .   .   .

There is a pleasure in the pathless woods,
There is a rapture on the lonely shore,
There is society, where none intrudes,
By the deep Sea, and music in its roar:
I love not Man the less, but Nature more,
From these our interviews, in which I steal
From all I may be, or have been before,
To mingle with the Universe, and feel
What I can ne'er express, yet cannot all conceal.

Naturalistic Humanism

Corliss Lamont

Humanism is such a warm and attractive word that in the 20th century it has been adopted by various groups, often diametrically opposed in ideology, whose use of it is most questionable. Even the Catholics, who still adhere to every outworn myth of Christian supernaturalism, promote what they call *Catholic Humanism;* while the Marxists, who reject in practice political democracy and civil liberties, continually talk of *Socialist Humanism.*

But the Humanism that has become increasingly influential in this century, in English-speaking countries and throughout the non-Communist world, is *naturalistic Humanism.* This is the Humanism that I have supported through the written and spoken word for some forty years.

To define naturalistic Humanism in a nutshell: it rejects all forms of supernaturalism, pantheism, and metaphysical idealism, and considers man's supreme aim as working for the welfare and progress of all humanity in this one and only life, according to the methods of reason, science and democracy.

To become more specific, Humanism believes first, that Nature or the universe makes up the totality of existence and is completely self-operating according to natural law, with no need for a God or gods to keep it functioning. This cosmos, unbounded in space and infinite in time, consists fundamentally of a constantly changing system of matter and energy, and is neutral in regard to man's well-being and values.

Second, Humanism holds that the race of man is the present culmination of a time-defying evolutionary process on this planet that has lasted billions of years: that man exists as an inseparable

149

unity of mind and body, and that therefore after death there can be no personal immortality or survival of consciousness.

Third, in working out its basic views on man and the universe, Humanism relies on reason, and especially on the established facts, laws, and methods of modern experimental science. In general, men's best hope for solving their problems is through the use of intelligence and scientific method applied with vision and determination. Such qualities as courage, love and perseverance provide emotional drive for successfully coping with difficulties, but it is reason that finds the actual solution.

Fourth, Humanism is opposed to all theories of universal determinism, fatalism or predestination and believes that human beings possess genuine freedom of choice (free will) in making decisions both important and unimportant. Free choice is conditioned by inheritance, education, the external environment (including economic conditions), and other factors. Nonetheless, it remains real and substantial. Humanism rejects both Marxist economic determinism and Christian theistic determinism. It places on the individual full responsibility for his decisions and actions.

Fifth, Humanism advocates an ethics or morality that grounds all human values in this-earthly experiences and relationships, and that views man as a functioning unity of physical, emotional and intellectual faculties. The Humanist holds as his highest ethical goal the this-worldly happiness, freedom, and progress—economic, cultural, and material—of all mankind, irrespective of race, religion, sex, or economic status. Reserving the word *love* for his family and friends, he has an attitude of *compassionate concern* toward his fellow men in general.

Sixth, in the controversial realm of sex relations, Humanism rejects entirely dualistic theories that separate soul from body and claim that the highest morality is to keep the soul pure and undefiled from physical pleasure and desire. The Humanist regards sexual emotions and their fulfillment as healthy, beautiful, and Nature's wonderful way of making possible the continued reproduction of the human race. While Humanism advocates high standards of conduct between the sexes, it rejects the puritanism of the past and looks upon sex love and sex pleasure as among the greatest of human experiences and values.

Seventh, Humanism believes that every individual must exercise a considerable amount of self-interest, if only to keep alive and healthy, but that altruistic endeavors on behalf of the community can be harmoniously combined with normal self-interest. Thus the good life is best attained by uniting the more personal satisfactions with important work and other activities that contribute to the welfare of one's city, nation or other social unit. Significant work usually deepens a person's happiness.

Eighth, Humanism supports the widest possible development of the arts and the awareness of beauty, so that the aesthetic experience may become a pervasive reality in the life of men. The Humanist eschews the artificial distinction between the fine arts and the useful arts and asserts that the common objects of daily use should embody a fusion of utility and grace. The mass production of industrial goods by machinery need not necessarily defeat this aim. Among other things, Humanism calls for the planned architectural reconstruction of towns and cities throughout America, so that beauty may prevail in our urban life.

Ninth, Humanism gives special emphasis to man's appreciation of the beauty and splendor of Nature. The Humanist energetically backs the widespread efforts for conservation, for protection of wild life, and the campaign to maintain and extend ecological values. His keen responsiveness to every sort of natural beauty evokes in him a feeling of profound kinship with Nature and its myriad forms of life.

Tenth, for the actualization of human happiness and freedom everywhere on earth, Humanism advocates the establishment of international peace, democracy, and a high standard of living throughout the world. Humanists, in their concern for the welfare of all nations, peoples, and races, adopt William Lloyd Garrison's aphorism, "Our country is the world; our countrymen are all mankind." Humanism is international in spirit and scope.

Eleventh, Humanism believes that the best type of government is some form of political democracy, including full freedom of expression and civil liberties throughout all areas of economic, political, and cultural life. Reason and science are crippled unless they remain unfettered in the pursuit of truth. In the United States, the Humanist militantly supports the fundamental guarantees in the Bill of Rights.

Twelfth, Humanism, in accordance with scientific method, encourages the unending questioning of basic assumptions and convictions in every field of thought. This includes, of course, philosophy, naturalistic Humanism, and the 12 points I have outlined in this attempt at definition. Humanism is not a new dogma, but is a developing philosophy ever open to experimental testing, newly discovered facts, and more rigorous reasoning.

I do not claim that every Humanist will accept all of the 12 points I have suggested. Nor do all Humanists wish to use the phrase *naturalistic* Humanism. Some prefer the term *scientific* Humanism, *secular* Humanism, or *democratic* Humanism. There is also a large group who consider Humanism a *religion* and who find an institutional home in the Fellowship of Religious Humanists, with its quarterly journal, *Religious Humanism*. For my own part, I prefer to call naturalistic Humanism a philosophy or way of life.

Living

Arthur Wakefield Slaten

The highest value we know is human life, nobly lived. What may exist elsewhere is beyond our ken, but earth knows nothing so precious as character that is wrought in the white light of sane ideals. Too much have we sought after outer gods; we turn now to the god within, the one neglected deity. May we know the glory of self-control, the joy of self-realization, the peace that comes with self-conquest. Upon all stricken and struggling souls may there rise the dawn of a renewed hope. To all of us may there be given the calm that comes from courage. May age be granted patience, youth wisdom. And together may we build that which earth never yet has seen, the divine society of human souls whose hunger and thirst is for righteousness, and whose toil is for the high prizes of the spirit.

Clarence Darrow

All men do the best they can. But none meet life honestly and few heroically. But, do we want life? It is only by avoiding pain and seeking pleasure that life is preserved. It is a biological question as well as a question of fact. After all, finally, life is lost. Each one must work out one's own life, and is entitled to neither credit nor blame for working it out.

All thinkers have ever answered the questions about the meaning, plan, scheme, and end of all, the same: that there is no guide and no light. Constant activity is the only answer to the meaning of life.

The purpose of life is living. Men and women should get the most they can out of their lives. The smallest, the tiniest intellect may be quite as valuable to society as the largest. It may be still more valuable to itself; it may have all the capacity for enjoyment that the wisest has. The purpose of man is like the purpose of the pollywog—to wiggle along as far as he can without dying; or, to hang to life until death takes him.

Corliss Lamont

Except for the infinitesimal part of its career represented by a few countries during the last century or so, mankind has ever been confronted with the crushing hardships of an economy of scarcity and the ruinous blasts of a Nature mighty and untamed. Influenced to a great extent by this forbidding background, man early proceeded to invent the stern superstitions of traditional religion and puritanical morality. And since the weight of history and tradition hangs so heavy, it has been extraordinarily difficult to convince men that they have a right to enjoy wholeheartedly and without any sense of sin the natural goods of this world.

The major principle of any rational Humanism is that since we possess only this one life we should make the most of it in terms of an abundant and reasoned happiness, unmarred and unrestrained by the conscience-stricken suppressions of the past. Such a philosophy heartily welcomes all life-enhancing and healthy pleasures, from the rollicking joys of vigorous youth to the contemplative delights of mellowed age. This way of life draws no hard-fast line, sets up no confusing and corrupting dualism, between the personality or mind, on the one hand, and the body or physical organism on the other. For in whatever he does man is a living unity of personality and body, an interfunctioning oneness of mental, emotional and physical qualities. Thus it should be perfectly clear that the so-called goods of the spirit—of culture and art and responsible citizenship—are, like all other natural goods, an integral and indispensable part of the ideal life, the higher hedonism, for which Humanism stands.

Even if the general viewpoint of Humanism be accepted, there is still one danger. That is the widespread phenomenon of future-worship, a too great willingness to sacrifice the present welfare of people on behalf of some distant goal; and a too great tendency on the part of the individual himself to think of personal happiness in terms of tomorrow rather than of today. As the poets make plain, the time to live and to be glad is now.

Edgar Lee Masters

Edmund Pollard

I would I had thrust my hands of flesh
Into the disk-flowers bee-infested
Into the mirror-like core of fire
Of the light of life, the sun of delight.
For what are anthers worth or petals
Or halo-rays? Mockeries, shadows
Of the heart of the flower, the central flame!
All is yours, young passer-by;
Enter the banquet room with the thought;
Don't sidle in as if you were doubtful
Whether you're welcome—the feast is yours!
Nor take but a little, refusing more
With a bashful "Thank you," when you're hungry.
Is your soul alive? Then let it feed!
Leave no balconies where you can climb:
Nor milk-white bosoms where you can rest;
Nor golden heads with pillows to share;
Nor wine cups while the wine is sweet;
Nor ecstasies of body or soul,
You will die, no doubt, but die while living
In depths of azure, rapt and mated,
Kissing the queen-bee, Life!

Omar Khayyam

A Book of Verses underneath the Bough,
A Jug of Wine, a Loaf of Bread——and Thou
    Beside me singing in the Wilderness——
Oh, Wilderness were Paradise enow!

Some for the Glories of This World; and some
Sigh for the Prophet's Paradise to come;
    Ah, take the Cash, and let the Credit go,
Nor heed the rumble of a distant Drum!

Ah, make the most of what we yet may spend,
Before we too into the Dust descend;
    Dust unto Dust, and under Dust to lie,
Sans Wine, sans Song, sans Singer, and——sans End!

Into this Universe, and *Why* not knowing
Nor *Whence,* like Water willy-nilly flowing;
    And out of it, as Wind along the Waste,
I know not *Whither,* willy-nilly blowing.

Oh, threats of Hell and Hopes of Paradise!
One thing at least is certain——*This* Life flies;
One thing is certain and the rest is Lies;
The Flower that once has blown for ever dies.

Denis Diderot

. . . . I am far from despising sensual pleasures. I have a palate too
and it is tickled by a delicate wine or dish; I have eyes and a heart
and I like to look at a pretty woman, like to feel the curve of her
breast under my hand, press her lips to mine, drink bliss from her
eyes and die of ecstasy in her arms. Sometimes a gay party with

my friends, even if it becomes a little rowdy, is not displeasing to me. But I must confess that I find it infinitely sweeter to succor the unfortunate, to disentangle a bad business, to give helpful advice, to read some pleasant book, to take a walk with a man or woman who is dear to me, to spend a few instructive hours with my children, to write a page of good prose, to carry out my duties, or to tell her whom I love something tender and true which brings her arms about my neck.

Roger E. Greeley

Living religiously does not involve conquering the universe or doing very great things. It begins with the conquest of the self, the refinement of character, the control of one's person in all of the interpersonal relationships that comprise life. Living is a series of approximations interrupted by lapses and failures. We can move in the proximity of our ideals only when idealism is the governing principle of our lives. Let us chart our wayfaring by the brightest stars that we can perceive and never allow the challenges of living to diminish their brilliance.

Living with Uncertainty

Sherwin Wine

The age of science is the age of uncertainty. No more eternal answers console the human heart. No more changeless doctrines pacify the human mind. Religious dogma has been replaced by the humility of testing. Mythical fantasy has yielded to the stingy help of public experience.

The age of science is the age of courage. Bravery is not possible when all is predictable. Only the danger of surprise gives persons the dignity of true freedom. The hero of modern times is no fanatic believer. He is the person of patience who is strong enough to live with uncertainty. He is the person of integrity who is honest enough to wait for what he cannot totally explain.

Human Significance

John Dewey

Men move between extremes. They conceive of themselves as gods, or feign a powerful and cunning god as an ally who bends the world to do their bidding and meet their wishes. Disillusionized, they disown the world that disappoints them; and hugging ideals to themselves as their own possession, stand in haughty aloofness apart from the hard course of events that pays so little heed to our hopes and aspirations. But a mind that has opened itself to experience and that has ripened through its discipline knows its own littleness and impotencies; it knows that its wishes and acknowledgements are not final measures of the universe whether in knowledge or in conduct, and hence are, in the end, transient. But it also knows that its juvenile assumption of power and achievement is not a dream to be wholly forgotten. It implies a unity with the universe that is to be preserved. The belief, and the effort of thought and struggle which it inspires, are also the doing of the universe, and they in some way, however slight, carry the universe forward. A chastened sense of our importance, apprehension that it is not a yardstick by which to measure the whole, is consistent with the belief that we and our endeavors are significant not only for themselves but in the whole.

Faith

Eric Hoffer

Faith in a holy cause is to a considerable extent a substitute for the lost faith in ourselves. . . . The less justified a man is in claiming excellence for his own self, the more ready is he to claim all excellence for his nation, his religion, his race or his holy cause.

*   *   *

A generation that wearies of technology is bound to turn to magic. Those who refuse to use machines that move mountains will pray for a faith that moves mountains.

Destiny and Design

Sigmund Freud

It seems not to be true that there is a power in the universe which watches over the well-being of every individual with parental care and brings all his concerns to a happy ending. On the contrary, the destinies of man are incompatible with a universal principle of benevolence or with—what is to some degree contradictory—a universal principle of justice. Earthquakes, floods and fires do not differentiate between the good and devout man and the sinner and unbeliever. And, even if we leave inanimate nature out of the account and consider the destinies of individual men in so far as they depend on their relations with others of their own kind, it is by no means the rule that virtue is rewarded and wickedness punished, but it happens often enough that the violent, the crafty and the unprincipled seize the desirable goods of the earth for themselves, while the pious go empty away. Dark, unfeeling and unloving powers determine human destiny. . . .

Robert Green Ingersoll

Design does not prove creation. You find the planets arranged in accordance with what you call a plan. That does not prove that they were created. It may prove that they are governed, but it certainly does not prove that they were created. Is it consistent to say that a design cannot exist without a designer but that a designer can? Does not a designer need a design as much as a design needs a designer? Does not a Creator need a Creator as much as the thing we think has been created?

Man in his ignorance supposed that all phenomena were produced by some intelligent powers with direct reference to him.

These religious people see nothing but design everywhere, and personal intelligent interference in everything. They insist that the universe has been created, and that the adaptation of means to ends is perfectly apparent. They point us to the sunshine, to the flowers, to the April rain, and to all there is of beauty and of use in the world. Did it ever occur to them that a cancer is as beautiful in its development as is the reddest rose? That what they are pleased to call the adaptation of means to ends, is as apparent in the cancer as in the April rain? How beautiful the process of digestion. By what ingenious methods the blood is poisoned so that the cancer shall have food! By what wonderful contrivances the entire system of man is made to pay tribute to this divine and charming cancer! What beautiful colors it presents! Seen through the microscope it is a miracle of order and beauty. All the ingenuity of man cannot stop its growth. Think of the amount of thought it must have required to invent a way by which the life of one man might be given to produce one cancer. Is it possible to look upon it and doubt that there is a design in the universe, and that the inventor of this wonderful cancer must be infinitely powerful, ingenious and good?

Nature is but an endless series of efficient causes. She cannot create but she eternally transforms. There was no beginning and there can be no end.

From Copernicus we learned that this earth is only a grain of sand on the infinite shore of the universe; that everywhere we are surrounded by shining worlds vastly greater than our own, all moving and existing in accordance with law. True, the earth began to grow small, but man began to grow great.

Can we find "design" in the fact that every animal lives upon some other—that every drop of every sea is a battlefield where the strong devours the weak? Over the precipice of cruelty rolls a perpetual Niagara of blood. Is there "design" in this?

Creativity and Creation

Sherwin Wine

Old rituals are comforting. They are familiar and predictable. They are safe and secure. They relieve us of the pain of continuous surprise. They reflect the mood of stability and eternity. Old rituals help us relax because they require no more exertion than the effort of repetition.

But endless repetition is dull, just as people without imagination are boring. Imitation and conformity are necessary for survival. They are not enough for happiness. Successful people are creative people. They refuse to accept the world as fixed. They refuse to believe that life offers only one script for living. They see old things and imagine new ways of putting them together. They see new things and fancy old settings which they will transform. They gaze at one scene and envision a hundred ways to describe it. They experience one life and imagine a thousand ways to live it.

Robert Green Ingersoll

The statement that in the beginning God created the heaven and the earth, I cannot accept. It is contrary to my reason, and I cannot believe it. It appears reasonable to me that force has existed from eternity. Force cannot, as it appears to me, exist apart from matter. Force, in its nature, is forever active, and without matter it could not act; and so I think matter must have existed forever. To conceive of matter without force, or of force without matter, or of a time when neither existed, or of a being who existed for an eternity without either and who out of nothing created both, is to me utterly impossible.

163

PART VIII

Reason and Rationality

Reason and Rationality

Reason is a paramount value in Humanism. It always has been, and it always will be central to Humanist philosophy and thought. Many a Humanist would maintain that reason is the single most important characteristic of Humanism. From the great classical Humanist philosophers to the contributions in this century of Bertrand Russell and Julian Huxley (to mention just two), reason is always in the forefront. Reason is inseparable from science. While the fundamentalists insist that only when you "embrace the impossible, the unreasonable, the illogical, can you be saved," Humanists respond with a view totally incompatible with blind faith. Humanists insist that reason is the pathway to growth and understanding and that blind faith closes the door on investigation and precludes progress by our species here and now.

Scholasticism sought to accommodate both reason and faith by declaring that you go as far as you can with reason and after this faith must take over. Humanists see no reason to accept this view offered by the medieval scholastics. Humanists are not moved to faith (blind or otherwise) by the existence of unknowns, of things we cannot explain or do not fully understand. Humanists in this circumstance say very simply, "We do not know." Those who cannot accept knowledge that is incomplete and the uncertainty it poses close the gaps in human knowledge with blocks of faith, cemented in place with the mortar of supernaturalism. Within this artificial compound, this illusory enclosure, they live in confidence that they have protected themselves from any unknown, malevolent happenings.

For the "faithful," on the loom of the fearful is woven the invisible tapestry of benevolent supernaturalism that is then hung in every edifice dedicated to "God." Supernaturalism pretends to be a pathway to places beyond the reach of reason. Humanists are willing to wait patiently as bit by bit, piece by piece we unlock secrets and create new truths and understandings concerning all species and the universe at large. Supernaturalistic faith urges the faithful to fly over the unknown to the comforting realm of the omnipotent "God." On the other hand, for Humanists, if something is reasonable, requires reason, is rational or exalts rationality, it is worthy of their concern, attention, and involvement. The enfranchisement of the human mind is a primary cause to which Humanists are dedicated. At the same time, Humanists can live in the here and now without all the answers. Humanists will follow wherever reason may lead and even though it may be but a foot at a time. For Humanists, worse than not knowing is pretending that through faith you do know. For this, in truth, can close the door to further inquiry and the discovery of the real truth. As H. L. Mencken observed, "Faith is belief in what we do not know while belief is faith in what we do know."

Reason and Harmony

Erich Fromm

What is essential in the existence of man is the fact that he has emerged from the animal kingdom, from instinctive adaptation, that he has transcended nature—although he never leaves it; he is a part of it—and yet once torn away from nature, he cannot return to it; once thrown out of paradise—a state of original oneness with nature—cherubim with flaming swords block his way, if he should try to return. Man can only go forward by developing his reason, by finding a new harmony, a human one, instead of the prehuman harmony which is irretrievably lost.

Authority

Walter Lippmann

But the teachers of Humanism have no credentials. Their teaching is not certified. They have to prove their case by the test of mundane experience. They speak with no authority which can be scrutinized once and for all, and then forever accepted. They cannot command. . . . They can only inquire, infer, and persuade. They have only human insight to guide them and those to whom they speak must in the end themselves accept the full responsibility for the consequences of any advice they choose to accept.

Truth and Falsehood

Robert Green Ingersoll

Let us be honest. Let us preserve the veracity of our souls. Let education commence in the cradle—in the lap of the loving mother. This is the first school. The teacher, the mother, should be absolutely honest.

The nursery should not be an asylum for lies.

Parents should be modest enough to be truthful—honest enough to admit their ignorance. Nothing should be taught as true that cannot be demonstrated.

Many people imagine that falsehoods may become respectable on account of age, that a certain reverence goes with antiquity, and that if a mistake is covered with the moss of sentiment it is altogether more credible than a parvenu fact. They endeavor to introduce the idea of aristocracy into the world of thought, believing—and honestly believing—that a falsehood long believed is far superior to a truth that is generally denied.

A lie will not fit a fact. It will only fit another lie made for the purpose. The life of a lie is simply a question of time. Nothing but truth is immortal.

Reason

Bertrand Russell

Until the deep conflicts of nations and classes which infect our world have been resolved, it is hardly to be expected that mankind will return to a rational habit of mind. The difficulty is that so long as unreason prevails, a solution of our troubles can only be reached by chance; for while reason, being impersonal, makes universal cooperation possible, <u>unreason,</u> since it represents private passions, <u>makes strife inevitable.</u> It is for this reason that rationality, in the sense of an appeal to a universal and impersonal standard of truth, is of supreme importance to the well-being of the human species.

Progress

John H. Dietrich

I need not speak to you of the far-off origin of the solar system from stardust and nebula, as a result of the working of natural conditions upon ever-existent force and matter. I need not speak of the cooling of our planet until it had formed a solid crust, nor of the appearance of vegetable life, followed by animal life. I need not speak of the progressive development of this life into higher and higher forms until at last it reached the stature of man; but let me speak of man who has been on this planet for several hundred thousand years at the very least. There never has been any Garden of Eden, or perfect condition in the past, there never has been any fall, there has been a constant rise. Man has been climbing slowly up the ages from the most primitive condition to the present civilization. There was a time when he was without the knowledge of fire, when he had no weapons or implements of any kind, except perhaps a limb torn from a tree. Later he began to break the rocks into shapes to use, making arrow heads and hatchets and spears. With these tools he began to dig out logs and make boats out of them. Then he discovered a method by which he could kindle a fire, and he smelted ores with which he made better implements, and invented the manufacture of rude kinds of pottery.

By and by, speech, partly an inheritance and partly an invention, widened its range and he learned to write in some crude fashion. Later he invented an alphabet and then he began to be civilized. He could now keep a record of the past so that the human race began to have a memory, and comparing its conditions with those of the past, it could forecast and trace out the steps of its advance. Then rude songs began to be sung and there was the beginning of a literature, and later metals of one kind and another came into use. Then some man invented moveable type, and the modern world with its literature became a possibility. And all this time from the beginning men were learning the rudiments of morals. For what are morals? Morals are nothing more or less than the rules wrought out as the result of human experience by means of which people are able to live together. Men have learned what is right and wrong in their relation to one another just as they have learned what is poison and what is healthful to eat—by experience. There is no need of a supernatural revelation to tell men that they must not kill. If people are to own anything, stealing must not be permitted. So every one of the principles of ethics has been wrought out naturally as the result of human experience.

And all this while men have been learning to care for the beautiful. From the first rude sketches on the wall of a cave, men have developed the finest artistic productions of painting and sculpture; and out of the crude noises and the sense of rhythm has come all the music of the world, until at last we have the great symphonies and oratorios and operas of the masters. Likewise man has developed as a religious creature. From the first fear of the natural powers and his desire to escape their wrath have grown all the religious systems of the world, until man has come to feel himself akin to the life and power of the universe. So step by step up the ages man has marched toward a higher civilization. This is the way the world has grown into its present shape; and we are still only in the beginning of our long march. Man is not yet really civilized. It is only the dawn. The sun's rays are striking here and there upon the hilltops, the light is breaking on some of the plateaus, but the great lowlands are still filled with the blackness of night, the awful darkness which precedes the dawn. The midday, when the sun's rays will penetrate into the deepest valleys and flood the whole earth with light, lies far beyond.

Positivism

Auguste Comte

The positive philosophy is the first that has ascertained the true point of view of social morality. The metaphysical philosophy sanctioned egotism; and the theological subordinated real life to an imaginary one while the new philosophy takes social morality for the basis of its whole system. The two former systems were so little favorable to the rise of the purely disinterested affections, that they often led to a dogmatic denial of their existence. . . . We have yet to witness the moral superiority of a philosophy which connects each of us with the whole of human existence, in all times and places. The restriction of our expectations to actual life must furnish new means of connecting our individual development with the universal progression, the growing regard to which will afford the only possible, and the utmost possible, satisfaction to our natural aspiration after eternity. For instance, the scrupulous respect for human life, which has always increased with our social progression, must strengthen more and more as the chimerical hope dies out which disparages the present life as merely accessory to the one in prospect. . . . By its various aptitudes, positive morality will tend more and more to exhibit the happiness of the individual as depending on the complete expansion of benevolent acts and sympathetic emotions towards the whole of our race; and even beyond our race, by a gradual extension to all sentient beings below us, in proportion to their animal rank and their social utility. The relative nature of the new philosophy will render it applicable, with equal facility and accuracy, to the exigencies of each case, individual or social, whereas we see how the absolute character of religious morality has deprived it of almost all force in cases which, arising after its institution, could not have been duly provided for. Till the full national establishment of positive morality has taken place, it is the business of true philosophers, ever the precursors of their race, to confirm it in the estimation of the world by the sustained superiority of their own conduct, personal, domestic, and social. . . .

Miracles

Robert Green Ingersoll

The real miracles are the facts in nature. . . . Believers in miracles should not endeavor to explain them. There is but one way to explain anything, and that is to account for it by natural agencies. The moment you explain a miracle, it disappears.

Kindness and Veracity

Bertrand Russell

When I try to discover what are the original sources of my opinions, both practical and theoretical, I find that most of them spring ultimately from admiration for two qualities—kindly feelings and veracity. To begin with kindly feeling: most of the social and political evils of the world arise through absence of sympathy and presence of hatred, envy, or fear. . . . Every kind of hostile action or feeling provokes a reaction by which it is increased and so generates a progeny of violence and injustice which has a terrible vitality. This can only be met by cultivating in ourselves and attempting to generate in the young feelings of friendliness rather than hostility, of well-wishing rather than malevolence, and of cooperation rather than competition.

If I am asked "Why do you believe this?" I should not appeal to any supernatural authority, but only to the general wish for happiness. A world full of hate is a world full of sorrow. From the point of view of worldly wisdom, hostile feeling and limitation of sympathy are folly. Their fruits are war, death, oppression, and torture, not only for their original victims but, in the long run, also for their perpetrators or their descendants. Whereas if we could all learn to love our neighbors the world would quickly become a paradise for us all.

Veracity, which I regard as second only to kindly feeling, consists broadly in believing according to evidence and not because a belief is comfortable or a source of pleasure. In the absence of veracity, kindly feeling will often be defeated by self-deception. . . . Veracity, or love of truth, is defined by Locke as "not entertaining any proposition with greater assurance than the proofs it is built upon will warrant." This definition is admirable in regard to all those

178

matters as to which proof may reasonably be demanded. But since proofs need premises, it is impossible to prove anything unless some things are accepted without proof. We must therefore ask ourselves: What sort of thing is it reasonable to believe without proof? I should reply: The facts of sense-experience and the principles of mathematics and logic—including the inductive logic employed in science. These are things which we can hardly bring ourselves to doubt and as to which there is a large measure of agreement among mankind. But in matters as to which men disagree, or as to which our own convictions are wavering, we should look for proofs, or, if proofs cannot be found, we should be content to confess ignorance.

There are some who hold that veracity should have limitations. Some beliefs, they say, are both comforting and morally beneficial, although it cannot be said that there are valid scientific grounds for supposing them to be true; these beliefs, they say, should not be critically examined. I cannot myself admit any such doctrine. I cannot believe that mankind can be the better for shrinking from the examination of this or that question. No sound morality can need to be based upon evasion, and a happiness derived from beliefs not justified on any ground except their pleasantness is not a kind of happiness that can be unreservedly admired.

These considerations apply especially to religious beliefs. Most of us have been brought up to believe that the universe owes its existence to an all-wise and all-powerful Creator, whose purposes are beneficent even in what to us may seem evil. I do not think it is right to refuse to apply to this belief the kind of tests that we should apply to one that touches our emotions less intimately and profoundly. Is there any evidence of the existence of such a Being? Undoubtedly belief in Him is comforting and sometimes has some good moral effects on character and behavior. But this is no evidence that the belief is true. For my part, I think the belief lost whatever rationality it once possessed when it was discovered that the earth is not the center of the universe. So long as it was thought that the sun and the planets and the stars revolved about the earth, it was natural to suppose that the universe had a purpose connected with the earth, and, since man was what man most admired on the earth, this purpose was supposed to be embodied in man. But astronomy and geology have changed all this. The earth is a minor planet of a minor star which is one of many millions of stars in a galaxy which is one of many millions of galaxies. Even within the life of our own planet man is only a brief interlude. Nonhuman life existed for countless ages before man was evolved. Man, even if he does not commit scientific suicide, will perish ultimately through failure of water or air or warmth. It is difficult to believe that Omnipotence needed so vast a setting for so small and transitory a result. . . .

There is a different and vaguer conception of cosmic Purpose as not omnipotent but slowly working its way through a recalcitrant material. This is a more plausible conception than that of a God who, though omnipotent and loving, has deliberately produced beings so subject to suffering and cruelty as the majority of mankind. I do not pretend to know that there is no such Purpose; my knowledge of the universe is too limited. But I do say, and I say with confidence, that the knowledge of other human beings is also limited, and that no one can adduce any good evidence that cosmic processes have any purpose whatever. Our very inadequate evidence, so far as it goes, tends in the opposite direction. . . .

Immortality, if we could believe in it, would enable us to shake off this gloom about the physical world. We should say that although our souls, during their sojourn here on earth, are in bondage to matter and physical laws, they pass at death into an eternal world beyond the empire of decay which science seems to reveal in the sensible world. But it is impossible to believe this unless we think that a human being consists of two parts—soul and body—which are separable and can continue independently of each other. Unfortunately all the evidence is against this. The mind grows like the body; like the body it inherits characteristics from both parents; it is affected by diseases of the body and by drugs; it is intimately connected with the brain. There is no scientific reason to suppose that after death the mind or soul acquires an independence of the brain which it never had in life. I do not pretend that this argument is conclusive, but it is all that we have to go upon except the slender evidence supplied by psychical research.

Many people fear that, without the theoretical beliefs that I find myself compelled to reject, the ethical beliefs which I accept could not survive. They point to the growth of cruel systems opposed to Christianity. But these systems, which grew up in a Christian atmosphere, could never have grown up if either kindly feeling or veracity had been practiced; they are evil myths, inspired by hate and without scientific support. . . . The reasons for the ethic that, in common with many whose benefits are more orthodox, I wish to see prevail are reasons derived from the course of events in this world. We have seen a great system of cruel falsehood, the Nazi system, lead a nation to disaster at immense cost to its opponents. It is not by such systems that happiness is to be achieved; even without the help of revelation it is not difficult to see that human welfare requires a less ferocious ethic. More and more people are becoming unable to accept traditional beliefs. If they think that, apart from these beliefs, there is no reason for kindly behavior the results may be needlessly unfortunate. That is why it is important to show that no supernatural reasons are needed to make men kind and to prove that only through kindness can the human race achieve happiness.

Intelligence

John Dewey

A moral law, like a law in physics, is not something to swear by and stick to at all hazards; it is a formula of the way to respond when specified conditions present themselves. Its soundness and pertinence are tested by what happens when it is acted upon. Its claim or authority rests finally upon the imperativeness of the situation that has to be dealt with, not upon its own intrinsic nature.

The blunt assertion that every moral situation is a unique situation having its own irreplaceable good may seem not merely blunt but preposterous. For the established tradition teaches that it is precisely the irregularity of special cases which makes necessary the guidance of conduct by universals, and that the essence of the virtuous disposition is willingness to subordinate every particular case to adjudication by a fixed principle. It would then follow that submission of a generic end and law to determination by the concrete situation entails complete confusion and unrestrained licentiousness. Let us, however, follow the pragmatic rule, and in order to discover the meaning of the idea ask for its consequences. Then it surprisingly turns out that the primary significance of the unique and morally ultimate character of the concrete situation is to transfer the weight and burden of morality to intelligence. It does not destroy responsibility; it only locates it. A moral situation is one in which judgment and choice are required antecedently to overt action. The practical meaning of the situation—that is to say the action needed to sastisfy it—is not self-evident. It has to be searched for. There are conflicting desires and alternative apparent goods. What is needed is to find the right course of action, the right good.

Doubt

Robert Weston

Cherish your doubts, for doubt is the handmaiden of truth. Doubt is the key to the door of knowledge; it is the servant of discovery. A belief that may not be questioned binds us to error, for there is incompleteness and imperfection in every belief. Let no man fear for truth, that doubt may consume it; for doubt is a testing of belief. He that would silence doubt is filled with fear. Let us not fear doubt, but let us rejoice in its help. It is to the wise as a staff to the blind; doubt is the handmaiden of truth.

Free Will and Determinism

Norman Cousins

Ever since I was old enough to read books on philosophy, I have been intrigued by the discussion on the nature of man. The philosophers have been debating for years about whether man is primarily good or primarily evil, whether he is primarily altruistic or selfish, co-operative or competitive, gregarious or self-centered, whether he enjoys free will or whether everything is predetermined.

As far back as the Socratic dialogues in Plato, and even before that, man has been baffled about himself. He knows he is capable of great and noble deeds, but then he is oppressed with the evidence of great wrongdoing.

And so he wonders. I don't presume to be able to resolve the contradictions. In fact, I don't think we have to. It seems to me that the debates over good and evil in man, over free will and determinism, and over all the other contradictions—that this debate is a futile one. For man is a creature of dualism. He is both good and evil, both altruistic and selfish. He enjoys free will to the extent that he can make decisions in life, but he can't change his chemistry or his relatives or his physical endowments—all of which were determined for him at birth. And rather than speculate over which side of him is dominant, he might do well to consider what the contradictions and circumstances are that tend to bring out the good or evil, that enable him to be nobler and a responsible member of the human race. And so far as free will and determinism are concerned, something I heard in India on a recent visit to the subcontinent may be worth passing along. Free will and determinism, I was told, are like a game of cards. The hand that is dealt you represents determinism. The way you play your hand represents free will.

Now where does all this leave us? It seems to me that we ought to attempt to bring about and safeguard those conditions that tend to develop the best in man. We know, for example, that the existence of fear and man's inability to cope with fear bring about the worst in him. We know that what is true of man on a small scale can be true of society on a large scale. And today the conditions of fear in the world are, I'm afraid, affecting men everywhere. More than twenty-three hundred years ago, the Greek world, which had attained tremendous heights of creative intelligence and achievement, disintegrated under the pressure of fear. Today, too, if I have read the signs correctly in traveling around the world, there is great fear. There is fear that the human race has exhausted its margin for error and that we are sliding into another great conflict that will cancel out thousands of years of human progress. And people are fearful because they don't want to lose the things that are more important than peace itself—moral, democratic, and spiritual values.

The problem confronting us today is far more serious than the destiny of any political system or even of any nation. The problem is the destiny of man: first, whether we can make this planet safe for man; second, whether we can make it fit for him. This I believe— that man today has all the resources to shatter his fears and go on to the greatest golden age in history, an age which will provide the conditions for human growth and for the development of the good that resides within man, whether in his individual or his collective being. And he has only to mobilize his rational intelligence and his conscience to put these resources to work.

Education

George Leonard

Some people believe in witchcraft. These people, critics of modern education, hold that there once lived a great witch named John Dewey. This witch seduced all the millions of American parents (who, *of course,* were firmly committed to Greek, Latin, and philosophy) away from these scholarly pursuits to pragmatic education and life adjustment (which, *of course,* have nothing to do with the American spirit). According to these believers in witchcraft, all we have to do is hang John Dewey in effigy, and then every student in the United States will become an old-time scholar.

Now, I really don't have to tell you how ridiculous this is. When you get right down to it, there were really *never* many old-time scholars. The "good old days" in education is a nostalgic hoax. And the truth of the matter is this: If John Dewey had not been born, Americans, in a very real sense, would have had to invent him.

The educational policies which have become linked with the name of John Dewey and labeled "progressive education" actually began in a number of schools long before Dewey wrote on the subject.

Strenuous pragmatism has been the past genius of this nation; anti-intellectualism has been one of its side effects—which we now see as tragic. But pragmatism and anti-intellectualism were not invented by educators. They were planted and nurtured by our forefathers, who found the ability to repair a wagon wheel or to build a log cabin more valuable than the ability to parse a Latin sentence; by our grandfathers, who used calculation more than calculus to set up the first great production lines; and by our fathers, who perfected a business community in which social skills and salesmanship brought more cash rewards than did scholarship.

At this point, we should get one thing absolutely clear. Those who have sought to place the entire blame for our school lags on a small group of educational theorists have shown a singular lack of discernment. Furthermore, by striking at the wrong target, they have confused issues, created unnecessary bitterness, and dissipated our needed national energy. No, "educationists" (as you are sometimes called) did not seduce parents away from scholarship. We were all seduced together by the facts of life in America.

But times change, and these days they change with startling and frightening speed. New challenges come like thunder; and we must, as Toynbee has shown us, make lightning-fast new responses or else see our culture disappear down the drainpipe of history.

Suddenly, it seems it's no longer enough to be practical and well-adjusted—that doesn't keep the Atlas missile from blowing up on the launching pad if the electronic theory is haywire or the skilled craftsmanship is unskilled. Nor did being some of the nicest, most popular guys we've ever known give our political leaders the hard, clear insight needed to realize the psychological effect of a sputnik on the nations of the world.

Nor, again, was anyone in power able to see, some years back when all the facts were there pressing against the windowpanes of our complacency, that African colonialism was ending, that a continent was to be plunged into turmoil, that we would need daring, active new ways of coping with the situation.

Worse yet, all too many of us *today* will go about our business as usual, with our use of old attitudes and expectations, unable to comprehend that according to most experts a nuclear war (which will probably kill us—I mean *us personally*) is likely within the next ten years. It is likely unless we are able to make a new response to a new challenge—a response that will entail some quite new attitudes on the subject of international responsibility.

For our nation to make these new responses, we shall need education of a higher order than ever before imagined, education that gives us not only data but the interrelation of data, a vision of the patterns of history, of the web of modern technology.

Robert Green Ingersoll

Nothing should be taught in any school that the teacher does not know. Beliefs, superstitions, theories should not be treated like demonstrated facts. The child should be taught to investigate, not to believe. Too much doubt is better than too much credulity. So, children should be taught that it is their duty to think for themselves, to understand, and, if possible to know.

PART IX

Religion

Religion

Is Humanism a religion? Do we capitalize the H *in Humanism to establish it as a religion on an equal footing with Christianity or Judaism?*

Some contemporary Humanists are adamant in their refusal even to consider Humanism a religion. At the same time, many Humanists find no problem in treating Humanism as a religion. In fact, it is the preference of many Humanists to speak of themselves as "religious" Humanists. These men and women insist that objections to using the word religious *are overcome by the manner in which religion is defined. It is beyond dispute that historically all major religions have employed the word* God. *This indisputable fact has led some Humanists to reject the word* religion *right along with any concept of God. (We must admit that where God is concerned, the most we have are concepts, simply this and nothing more.)*

The religious Humanists nevertheless find no problem with the word religion. *They ask, "What if you define* religion *as the quest for the highest values in life and the conscious, reasoned attempt to live in the light of those values?" What if your definition declares: Religion is that which causes you to seek to live a creative life in the presence of annihilation, which is the end of life. And still another definition is: Religion is that which gives meaning in life even though life is temporal. Defined in these ways,* religion *is acceptable to many Humanists.*

Another objection to the terms religion *and* religious *is voiced by a number of church vs. state purists. These people would have Humanism divorced from religion because of problems that have resulted from recent U.S. Supreme Court decisions recognizing or declaring Humanism to be a religion. While sharing the concern of these church vs. state enthusiasts, I must ask if the stance of Humanists will change the Court's decisions. Unless the Court reverses itself, Humanism will remain a religion—in the eyes of the Court— regardless of what Humanists may decide.*

Regardless of the reader's opinion in this matter, Humanists cannot dismiss religion as a philosophical concern or unreality. This holds whether or not the individual Humanist cares to employ the word in the vocabulary of Humanism.

Humanism and Religion

Curtis W. Reese

The ethical life of Humanism, then, is based on the actual situation of human nature. We are not disembodied souls living in a world of pure spirit, nor do we in fact seek to be. We have appetites and passions, hungers and thirsts, desires and aspirations. We have aches and pains, as well as joys and excitements. We must eat and keep warm, as well as think and aspire. And all these are of the very texture of the moral situation. The Humanist ethic is not life in accord with an absolute standard that never knew reality on land or sea, but life in the fullness of the inherent and the unique needs of individual man in his social setting.

The Humanist gospel aims to satisfy the whole of human life, no phase of life being taboo. In most religions some of the deepest needs and most fruitful sources of abundant living, including the whole sweep of sex, have not only been ignored but actually repressed and positively condemned. But Humanism incorporates the physical as well as the spiritual in its very foundation.

But life is also freedom and loyalty and dreams and visions; and these are of the very texture of physical well-being, just as food and shelter and sex are of the very texture of spiritual well-being. Man cannot live by bread alone, nor can he live by visions alone. The soil of the earth blooms into the flowers of the spirit.

So Humanist religion plunges boldly into the thick of the battle for a full life for all mankind. It is interested in everything that concerns human life. The sweat of the shop and the grind of the marketplace, as well as the thoughts of philosophers and the dreams of seers. It sorrows over every wail of woe and rejoices over every far-flung hope. Sometimes grimly, sometimes buoyantly, but always definitely and with the rear bridges burned, Humanism tackles life situations. Issues shift, needs change, men grow old and pass away; but always there remains the human struggle to wring a satisfactory life from environing situations that are sometimes none too friendly. But with greater knowledge comes greater control, and with greater control more visions of far-reaching goals. With increasing knowledge and insight, with growing determination and power, man moves steadily forward, striking from his soul the chains that nature and his older self have forged, courageously facing the present, and venturing in the face of greatest difficulties to chart the unknown tomorrow.

*   *   *

. . . Of all the needs of the race, the greatest are for freedom from repression and oppression, and for committal to the fullest possible realization of life on the highest possible human plane.

Humanism is bound up with the full life. It is intimately concerned with all social instrumentalities; with education and politics, with science and art, with industries and homes. It seeks not only to interpret these but to guide them. It aims to direct all social instruments and powers to the ends of human life, and to create new instruments and powers of life. It regards the whole sweep of life—the sex life, the political life, the economic life—as within its province. It regards the proper world order as a religious order. The whole of life goes up or down together, and none of it is foreign to the interest of religion. When the purpose of thought and conduct is human well-being, such thought and conduct is religious in character.

Julian Huxley

I use the word *Humanist* to mean someone who believes that man is just as much a natural phenomenon as an animal or a plant, that his body, his mind, and his soul were not supernaturally created but are all products of evolution, and that he is not under the control or guidance of any supernatural Being or beings, but has to rely on himself and his own powers. And I use *faith* in the sense of a set of essentially religious beliefs.

How then can a Humanist be religious? Is not religion necessarily concerned with supernatural beings? The answer is "No." Religion of some sort seems always to have been a feature of man's life; but some religions are not concerned with God, and some not with any sort of supernatural beings at all. Religions are of many kinds, good and bad, primitive and advanced: but they all have one thing in common—they help man to cope with the problem of his place and role in the strange universe in which he lives.

Religion . . . always involves the sense of sacredness or reverence, and it is always concerned with what is felt to be more absolute, with what transcends immediate, particular, everyday experience. It aims at helping people to transcend their petty or selfish or guilty selves. All organized religions not only have a set of rituals but a moral code—what is right and what is wrong: and a system of beliefs. In the long run, the beliefs determine the moral code, and they in their turn are based on man's knowledge of himself and the world.

Humanist beliefs are based on human knowledge, especially on the knowledge-explosion of the hundred years since Darwin published *The Origin of Species,* which has revealed to us a wholly new picture of the universe and of our place in it. We now believe with confidence that the whole of reality is one gigantic process of evolution. This produces increased novelty and variety, and ever higher types of organization; in a few spots it has produced life; and, in a few of those spots of life, it has produced mind and consciousness.

This universal process is divisible into three phases or sectors, each with its own method of working, its own rate of change, and its own kind of results. Over most of the universe it is in the lifeless or inorganic phase. On earth (and undoubtedly on some planets of other suns) it is in the organic or biological phase. This works by natural selection and has produced a huge variety of animals and plants, some astonishingly high organizations (like our own bodies, or an ant colony), and the emergence of mind.

Finally man (and possibly a few other organisms elsewhere) has entered the human or, as we may call it, psychosocial phase, which is based on the accumulation of knowledge and the organization of experience. It works chiefly by a conscious selection of ideas and aims, and produces extremely rapid change. Evolution in this phase is mainly cultural, not genetic; it is no longer focused solely on survival, but is increasingly directed towards fulfillment and towards quality of achievement.

Man is the latest dominant type of life on this earth, and the sole agent for its further evolution. He is the product of more than two and a half million years of past evolution; and we believe that he has at least an equally vast span of future evolution before him.

Though human evolution has been accompanied by much evil and horror, it has led to real advances (for instance, in health and length of life), and has produced great new achievements (such as cathedrals and airplanes, poems and philosophies, arts and sciences). And this has been due to the increase of human experience and knowledge and its better organization in concepts and scientific laws, in ideas and works of art. We know that a large number of things that used to be supposed to be due to supernatural intervention are nothing of the sort, but are the result of perfectly natural causes. We do not believe that epidemics are divine punishments, or earthquakes divine warnings; we do not believe that witches are in league with the Devil, or that artistic inspiration comes from a supernatural source; prayers for rain are still offered in church, but very few people (and no Humanists) believe that God has any influence on the weather. We know that there is no hell full of devils inside the earth, and nothing like the traditional orthodox Christian idea of heaven up in the sky.

But we have faith in the capacities and possibilities of man: most immediately in his capacity to accumulate his experience, and in the resultant possibilities of increasing his knowledge and understanding. We have seen their results in science and medicine; we have faith in their possibilities for psychology and politics, for conservation and eugenics. But we must think of man's other capacities, too. His capacity for disinterested curiosity and wonder leads him both to seek and to enjoy knowledge. His capacity for enjoying beauty pushes him to create, to preserve, and to contemplate it. His capacity to feel guilt impels him towards morality, his sense of incompleteness leads him to seek greater wholeness. He is endowed with a sense of justice, which slowly but steadily brings about the remedying of injustice. He has a capacity for compassion which leads him to care for the sick, the aged, and the persecuted, and a capacity for love which could (and sometimes does) override his capacity for hate.

Many human possibilities are still unrealized save by a few: the possibility of enjoying experiences of transcendent rapture, physical and mystical, aesthetic and religious, or that of attaining an inner harmony and peace that puts a man above the cares and worries of daily life. Indeed man as a species has not yet realized more than a fraction of his possibilities of health, physical and mental, and spiritual well-being, of achievement and knowledge, of wisdom and enjoyment, or of satisfaction in participating in worthwhile or enduring projects, including that most enduring of all projects, man's further evolution.

So man's most sacred duty is to realize his possibilities of knowing, feeling, and willing to the fullest extent, in the development of human individuals, in the achievements of human societies, and in the evolution of the whole human species. I believe that an understanding of the extent to which man falls short of realizing his splendid possibilities will stimulate him to learn how they can be realized, and that this will be the most powerful religious motive in the next stage of our human evolution. As a Humanist, that is my faith.

Generalizations About Humanism

George E. Axtelle

It is commonly asserted that religion is a universal need, and that it is essential to both education and morals. Whether this is true depends upon what is meant by *religion*. If by *religion* is meant the orthodox beliefs in a Supreme Being, another world and an afterlife, it is obviously untrue. There are too many exceptions, people of great distinction morally and intellectually, who believed in none of these. If however we conceive of religion as certain cultural and psychological functions, the statement seems to be true.

Any people, to be a society, must have a cluster of common beliefs, values and practices, without which there would be no community. It is no accident that religion is so often associated with civilizations, for they are the "genius" of civilization. They provide perspective, purpose and meaning.

It may be asked, if this is true, how explain America with its plurality of religions? The answer is that with all the plurality of "denominations," we do have a body of belief, values and practices which we hold in common. Briefly these might be designated as science, industrialism and democracy. Actually our religion is still very much in the making.

Thomas Aquinas in the thirteenth century provided an intellectual, moral and political synthesis of his culture, which admirably expressed its deeper meanings. However, with the growth of trade, the developing interests in nature, and the emergence of scientific modes of thinking, it lost its ascendency. Had it had greater flexibility, it might have responded to the changes in culture and effected a religious continuity which would have given direction and purpose to the modern world without the serious religious upheavals.

It is my belief that each period of human culture requires a system of belief, value and practice which gives it integrity. At the same time it must be responsive and adaptive to its time if it is to remain relevant. Thus our future requires a religion which incorporates and integrates the moving forces of our time. This is to say it must reflect democracy, science, our economic and industrial life, and the arts and our cosmopolitan world, in such a way as to give our culture an integrated character. The integrity will not come from a theological imposition from above, but will be an integrity which comes from the actual unification of the various institutions and functions of our culture. Our devotion would thus be to the continued preservation and improvement of integrity under changing conditions. It would be a loyalty to whatever made for the increased vitality of both the culture and of individuals. Recognizing the culture as the instrument by means of which men live together effectively, with meaning and love, it would be concerned with the enhancement of human life.

Robert Green Ingersoll

Every church that has a standard higher than human welfare is dangerous.

True religion is not a theory—it is a practice. It is not a creed—it is a life. True religion is subordination of the passions to the perceptions of the intellect.

Religion has not civilized man—man has civilized religion.

Religion does not consist in worshipping gods, but in aiding the well-being, the happiness of man. No human being knows whether any god exists or not. All that has been said and written about "our god" or the gods of other people has no known fact or foundation. Words without thoughts, clouds without rain. Let us put theology out of religion.

Religion and morality have nothing in common, and yet there is no religion except the practice of morality. What you call religion is simply superstition.

Real religion means the doing of justice. Real religion means the giving to others every right you claim for yourself. Real religion consists in duties of man to man, in feeding the hungry, in clothing the naked, in defending the innocent, and in saying what you believe to be true.

A religion that does not command the respect of the greatest minds will, in a little while, excite the mockery of all.

Bertrand Russell

Fear is the basis of religious dogma, as of so much else in human life. Fear of human beings, individually or collectively, dominates much of our social life, but it is fear of nature that gives rise to religion. The antithesis of mind and matter is, as we have seen, more or less illusory; but there is another antithesis which is more important—that, namely, between things that can be affected by our desires, and things that cannot be so affected. The line between the two is neither sharp nor immutable—as science advances, more and more things are brought under human control. Nevertheless there remain things definitely on the other side. Among these are all the *large* facts of our world, the sort of facts that are dealt with by astronomy. It is only facts on or near the surface of the earth that we can, to some extent, mould to suit our desires. And even on the surface of the earth our powers are very limited. Above all, we cannot prevent death, although we can often delay it.

Religion is an attempt to overcome this antithesis. If the world is controlled by God, and God can be moved by prayer, we acquire a share in omnipotence. In former days, miracles happened in answer to prayer; they still do in the Catholic Church, but Protestants have lost this power. However, it is possible to dispense with miracles, since Providence has decreed that the operation of natural laws shall produce the best possible results. Thus belief in God still serves to humanize the world of nature, and to make men feel that physical forces are really their allies. In like manner immortality removes the terror from death. People who believe that when they die they will inherit eternal bliss may be expected to view death without horror, though, fortunately for medical men, this does not invariably happen. It does, however, soothe men's fears somewhat, even when it cannot allay them wholly.

Religion, since it has its source in terror, has dignified certain kinds of fear, and made people think them not disgraceful. In this it has done mankind a great disservice: *all* fear is bad. I believe that when I die I shall rot, and nothing of my ego will survive. I am not young, and I love life. But I should scorn to shiver with terror at the thought of annihilation. Happiness is none the less true happiness because it must come to an end, nor do thought and love lose their value because they are not everlasting. Many a man has borne himself proudly on the scaffold; surely the same pride should teach us to think truly about man's place in the world. Even if the open windows of science at first make us shiver after the cosy indoor warmth of traditional humanizing myths, in the end the fresh air brings vigour, and the great spaces have a splendour of their own.

H. L. Mencken

To sum up:
1. The cosmos is a gigantic flywheel making 10,000 revolutions a minute.
2. Man is a sick fly taking a dizzy ride on it.
3. Religion is the theory that the wheel was designed and set spinning to give him a ride.

Thomas Henry Huxley

The germ of Religion, arising, like all other kinds of knowledge, out of the action and interaction of man's mind, with that which is not man's mind, has taken the intellectual coverings of Fetishism or Polytheism; of Theism or Atheism; of Superstition or Rationalism.

With these, and their relative merits and demerits I have nothing to do; but this is needful for my purpose to say, that if the religion of the present differs from that of the past, it is because the theology of the present has become more scientific than that of the past; because it has not only renounced idols of wood and idols of stone, but begins to see the necessity of breaking in pieces the idols built up of books and traditions and finespun ecclesiastical cobwebs; and of cherishing the noblest and most human of man's emotions, by worship "for the most part of the silent sort" at the altar of the Unknown and the Unknowable . . .

. . . What are among the moral convictions most fondly held by barbarous and semi-barbarous people? They are the convictions that authority is the soundest basis of belief; that merit attaches to a readiness to believe; that the doubting disposition is a bad one, and skepticism a sin; that when good authority has pronounced what is to be believed, and faith has accepted it, reason has no further duty. There are many excellent persons who yet hold by these principles, and it is not my present business or intention to discuss their views. All I wish to bring clearly before your minds is the unquestionable fact that the improvement of natural knowledge is effected by methods which directly give the lie to all these convictions, and assume the exact reverse of each to be true.

The improver of natural knowledge absolutely refuses to acknowledge authority, as such. For him, skepticism is the highest of duties; blind faith the one unpardonable sin. And it cannot be otherwise, for every great advance in natural knowledge has involved the absolute rejection of authority, the cherishing of the keenest skepticism, the annihilation of the spirit of blind faith; and the most ardent votary of science holds his firmest conviction, not because the men he most venerates holds them; not because their verity is testified by portents and wonders; but because his experience teaches him that whenever he chooses to bring these convictions into contact with their primary source, nature—whenever he thinks fit to test them by appealing to experiment and to observation—nature will confirm them. The man of science has learned to believe in justification, not by faith, but by verification.

Julian Huxley

But if religion is not essentially belief in a God or Gods and obedience to their command or will, what then is it? It is a way of life, an art like other kinds of living, and an art which must be practiced like other arts if we are to achieve anything good in it.

Religious emotion will always exist, will always demand expression. The ways in which it finds expression may be good or may be bad: or, what seems hardly to have been realized, they may be on the whole good for the worshiper, but bad for the community. Man's scale of desires and values, his spiritual capacities, dictate the direction of his religion, the goal towards which it aspires; the facts of Nature and life dictate the limits within which it may move, the trellis on whose framework those desires and emotions must grow if they are to receive the beams of truth's sun, if they aspire above creeping on the ground. It is our duty to know those outer facts truly and completely, to be willing to face all truth and not to try to reject what does not tally with our desires: and it is our duty to realize our own capacities, to know what desires are to be put in command, what desires are to be harnessed to subordinate toil, to place our whole tumultuous life of feeling and will under the joint guidance of reverence and reason.

Insofar as we do this, we prevent the man of devout religious feeling from being subordinated to a system which may organize the spirit of religion in opposition to discovery or necessary change, or may discharge its power in cruelty or persecution; and we help religion to help the progress of civilization. But insofar as we neglect this, we are making man a house divided against itself, and allowing the strong tides of religious feeling to run to waste or to break in and devastate the fruit of man's labor. And the choice is in our own hands.

PART X

Science and the
Scientific Method

Science and the
Scientific Method

Speculative, pure science is often ridiculed and censured by the public at large. The public demands immediate application of whatever science is doing, to the ills of humanity right now. During the years immediately preceding the U.S. landing a man on the moon, much protest was raised, strident voices declaring that the whole investment was nothing but a scientific "boondoggle," a waste of the taxpayers' money.

Humanists have been and hopefully will remain in the forefront in promoting the continued good health of scientific inquiry in its purest form. One task for Humanists is to constantly make clear the distinction between pure science and technology. Even Einstein was criticized for his role in the development of the now primitive A-bomb. It was Einstein who was also responsible for a quiet but important revolution within the scientific community when he demanded that science assume responsibility for its actions. No longer would a scientist be able to claim that by virtue of residing in the ivory tower was one thus freed from any responsibility for the consequences of work, discoveries, or theories. Einstein made scientists accountable not only to the truth but also to humanity. If he did not succeed entirely in this crusade, he and Dr. Bronowski certainly did much to focus attention on science and social responsibility.

For centuries, science has been governed by the desire to be able to predict and control. In the well-established absence of any benevolent deity, humanity had better learn how to utilize science to better predict and control the environment, human numbers, and their quality, or else the future of homo sapiens *is indeed dim. The scientific method of empirical observation, reason, controlled experimentation, and hypothesizing is also part of responsible Humanism. Science has never been at war with religion by utilizing the scientific method. It is religion that has waged an endless war against science whenever a scientific disclosure refutes or destroys a theological "truth." Even in the last quarter of the twentieth century, science is under attack by those who insist that our only salvation lies in foolish ecumenism, and this has sometimes silenced criticism of antiscientific statements that are made by clerics. Humanism must take the lead in protecting an unfettered science and must champion an adjustment in our way of doing things where science has shown us to be in error. Science must be free to make any responsible inquiry it wishes. How science is best to serve humanity is quite another question, and our concern must be that Humanists continue to support pure science. We ought to applaud the Einsteins, the Bronowskis, the Huxleys, few though they may be and often forced to speak to a very small audience about very large matters.*

Science

Clyde Kluckhohn

Americans enlarged the meaning of freedom and gave it many new expressions.

It is this prospect for American culture which we must cherish and believe in. Nor is there anything in science which indicates that the dreams of man do not influence, nay sometimes determine his behavior. While choice is most often a flattering illusion, while antecedent and existent hard-sense data usually shape our destinies, there are moments in the careers of nations, as well as in the careers of individuals, when opposing external forces are about equally balanced, and it is then that intangibles like "will" and "belief" throw the scales. Cultures are not altogether self-contained systems which inevitably follow out their own self-determined evolution. Sorokin and other prophets of doom fail to see that one of the factors which determines the next step in the evolution of a system is precisely the dominant attitudes of people. And these are not completely determined by the existent culture. John Dewey has shown us that in "judgments of practice" the hypothesis itself has a crucial influence upon the course of events: "to the extent that it is seized and acted upon, it weights events in its favor."

Even that erstwhile pessimist, Aldous Huxley, has seen that the discoveries of modern psychology have been perverted to bolster a false determinism. If responses can be conditioned, they can by the same token be deconditioned and reconditioned--through neither individuals nor peoples change suddenly and completely. We are now released from the dominantly external and material demands which frontier conditions made upon our society. Intelligent planning can ease the hostile tensions of natural anarchy by providing both security and socialized freedom for the individual. Ideals of flourishing freshness that adapt to changed conditions and to what is sound and creative in the distinctive American Way are the only sure antidote for our social ills. Only those ideals will spread and be accepted which correspond to the culturally created emotional needs of the people. Scientific humanism is such an ideal. Rooted in the tradition of Americans to value scientific achievement highly, scientific humanism can actualize the American Dream. As our culture has come from all the world, so must we give back to all the world not that technological materialism which is science cheapened and debased but the scientific attitude woven into the stuff of people's daily lives. This is a vision of humility in the face of the complexity of things, of the joyous pursuit of ideas of which there is no exclusive possession. This is science not as the provider of the agencies of barbarism but science as revealing the order in experience, as heightening the sense of our precarious dependence one upon the other, as the surest and most powerful of internationalizing forces.

Scientific humanism should be the sturdy creed of the future. Despite uncritical worship of invention and technology, the masses are still, in Carlson's expression, "innocent of science, in the sense of the spirit and the method of science as part of their way of life. . . . Science in this sense has as yet hardly touched the common man or his leaders." An effective working majority of our citizens need no longer base their personal security upon expectation of future life or adult dependency upon the projected images of parent-persons. The scientific vision is the vision which Plato saw in the *Symposium,* a security system which is depersonalized but humanized rather than dehumanized. To try to make such a vision real offers American men and women that common nobility of purpose which is the vitalizing energy of any significant culture. The venture demands a courage analogous to religious faith, a courage undismayed by the failure of any specific experiment, a courage ready to offer the renunciations of waiting long, a courage which recognizes that even negative knowledge means growth, a courage realizing that the general hypotheses underlying the venture will be proved only if diminished anxiety and greater gusto in day-to-day living transform the lives of us all.

Lucretius

No single thing abides; but all things flow.
Fragment to fragment clings—the things thus grow
　　Until we know and name them. By degrees
They melt, and are no more the things we know.

Globed from the atoms falling slow or swift
I see the suns, I see the systems lift
　　Their forms; and even the systems and the suns
Shall go back slowly to the eternal drift.

You too, oh earth—your empires, lands, and seas—
Least with your stars, of all the galaxies,
　　Globed from the drift like these, like these you too
Shalt go. You are going, hour by hour, like these.

Nothing abides. The seas in delicate haze
Go off; those mooned sands forsake their place;
　　And where they are, shall other seas in turn
Mow with their scythes of whiteness other bays. . .

The seeds that once were we take flight and fly,
Winnowed to earth, or whirled along the sky,
　　Not lost but disunited. Life lives on.
It is the lives, the lives, the lives, that die.

They go beyond recapture and recall,
Lost in the all-indissoluble All:—
　　Gone like the rainbow from the fountain's foam,
Gone like the spindrift shuddering down the squall.

Flakes of the water, on the waters cease!
Soul of the body, melt and sleep like these.
　　Atoms to atoms—weariness to rest —
Ashes to ashes—hopes and fears to peace!

Science

O Science, lift aloud your voice that stills
The pulse of fear, and through the conscience thrills—
    Thrills through the conscience with the news of peace—
How beautiful your feet are on the hills!

John Dewey

Apologists for a religion often point to the shift that goes on in scientific ideas and materials as [being] evidence of the unreliability of science as a mode of knowledge. They often seem peculiarly elated by the great, almost revolutionary, change in fundamental physical conceptions that has taken place in science during the present generation. Even if the alleged unreliability were as great as they assume (or even greater), the question would remain: Have we any other recourse for knowledge? But in fact they miss the point. Science is not constituted by any particular body of subject matter. It is constituted by a method, a method of changing beliefs by means of tested inquiry as well as of arriving at them. It is its glory, not its condemnation, that its subject matter develops as the method is improved. There is no special subject matter of belief that is sacrosanct. The identification of science with a particular set of beliefs and ideas is itself a holdover of ancient and still current dogmatic habits of thought which are opposed to science in its actuality and which science is undermining.

For scientific method is adverse not only to dogma but to doctrine as well, provided we take *doctrine* in its usual meaning—a body of definite beliefs that need only to be taught and learned as true. This negative attitude of science to doctrine does not indicate indifference to truth. It signifies supreme loyalty to the method by which truth is attained. The scientific-religious conflict ultimately is a conflict between allegiance to this method and allegiance to even an irreducible minimum of belief so fixed in advance that it can never be modified.

Julian Huxley

There are many well-intentioned people today who will tell you that the conflict between science and religion is over. It is not so. What has been rather loosely called the conflict between science and religion is just reaching its acute phase. Up to the present the fighting has been an affair of outposts; the incidents of Galileo and Darwin were but skirmishes. The real conflict is to come: it concerns the very conception of Deity.

I say that the phrase "the conflict between science and religion" is a loose phrase. It is a loose phrase because the conflict is not really between science and religion at all, but between a certain kind of religion and some particular conclusions of science.

There are in reality several conflicts. One is between a certain religious tradition on the one hand, a tradition so encrusted with sanctity by long association that is mistaken for something essential to religion, and, on the other, a number of actual facts discovered by scientific investigators. Another conflict is that between the passion for getting at the truth that characterizes some great minds, including the highest type of scientific mind, and the tendency to assert and believe what we desire, which is found in so many human beings and so many religious beliefs. Still a third conflict is between the over-cautious or limited mind, scientific or other, and a certain too matter-of-fact kind of science, which persists in denying the truth or the value of what they cannot see or understand, and that side of rich human nature which is capable of a deep and vital religious experience.

At the present moment, organized religion happens to be arrayed, on the whole, against organized science. But the real conflicts are between bad, limited, or distorted religion and pure and high religion; and between limited and grudging science and science full and unafraid.

Infinity

John Dewey

One important incident of the new science was the destruction of the idea that the earth is the center of the universe. When the idea of a fixed center went, there went with it the idea of a closed universe and a circumscribing heavenly boundary. To the Greek sense, just because its theory of knowing was dominated by esthetic considerations, the finite was the perfect. Literally, the finite was the finished, the ended, the completed, that with no ragged edges and unaccountable operations. The infinite or limitless was lacking in character just because it was in-finite. Being everything, it was nothing. It was unformed and chaotic, uncontrolled and unruly, the source of incalculable deviations and accidents. Our present feeling that associates infinity with boundless power, with capacity for expansion that knows no end, with the delight in a progress that has no external limit, would be incomprehensible were it not that interest has shifted from the esthetic to the practical; from interest in beholding a harmonious and complete scene to interest in transforming an inharmonious one. One has only to read the authors of the transition period, says Giordano Bruno, to realize what a pent-in, suffocating sensation they associated with a closed, finite world, and what a feeling of exhilaration, expansion, and boundless possiblity was aroused in them by the thought of a world infinite in stretch of space and time, and composed internally of infinitesimal, infinitely numerous elements. That which the Greeks withdrew from with repulsion they welcomed with an intoxicated sense of adventure. The infinite meant, it was true, something forever untraversed even by thought, and hence something forever unknown—no matter how great [an] attainment in learning. But this "forever unknown," instead of being chilling and repelling, was now an inspiring challenge to ever-renewed inquiry and an assurance of inexhaustible possibilities of progress.

Evolution

Charles Darwin

Natural selection follows from the struggle for existence; and this from a rapid rate of increase. It is impossible not to regret bitterly, but whether wisely is another question, the rate at which man tends to increase; for this leads in barbarous tribes to infanticide and many other evils, and in civilized nations to abject poverty, celibacy, and to the late marriages of the prudent. But as man suffers from the same physical evils as the lower animals, he has no right to expect an immunity from the evils consequent on the struggle for existence. Had he not been subjected during primeval times to natural selection, assuredly he would never have attained to his present rank. Since we see in many parts of the world enormous areas of the most fertile land capable of supporting numerous happy homes, but peopled only by a few wandering savages, it might be argued that the struggle for existence had not been sufficiently severe to force man upwards to his highest standard. Judging from all we know of man and the lower animals, there has always been sufficient variability in their intellectual and moral faculties, for a steady advance through natural selection. No doubt such advance demands many favorable concurrent circumstances; but it may well be doubted whether the most favorable would have sufficed, had not the rate of increase been rapid, and the consequent struggle for existence extremely severe. It even appears from what we see, for instance, in parts of South America, that a people which may be called civilized, such as the Spanish settlers, is liable to become indolent and to retrograde, when the conditions of life are very easy. With highly civilized nations continued progress depends in a subordinate degree on natural selection; for such nations do not supplant and exterminate one another as do savage tribes.

216

Nevertheless the more intelligent members within the same community will succeed better in the long run than the inferior, and leave a more numerous progeny, and this is a form of natural selection. The more efficient causes of progress seem to consist of a good education during youth whilst the brain is impressible, and of a high standard of excellence, inculcated by the ablest and best men, embodied in the laws, customs, and traditions of the nation, and enforced by public opinion. It should, however, be borne in mind, that the enforcement of public opinion depends upon our appreciation of the approbation and disapprobation of others; and this appreciation is founded on our sympathy, which it can hardly be doubted was originally developed through natural selection as one of the most important elements of the social instincts.

Change

John Dewey

Instead of a closed universe, science now presents us with one infinite in space and time, having no limits here or there, at this end, so to speak, or at that, and as infinitely complex in internal structure as it is infinite in extent. Hence it is also an open world, an infinitely variegated one, a world which in the old sense can hardly be called a universe at all; so multiplex and far-reaching that it cannot be summed up and grasped in any one formula. And change rather than fixity is now a measure of "reality" or energy of being; change is omnipresent. The laws in which the modern man of science is interested are laws of motion, of generation and consequence. He speaks of law where the ancients spoke of kind and essence, because what he wants is a correlation of changes, an ability to detect one change occurring in correspondence with another. He does not try to define and delimit something remaining constant in change. He tries to describe a constant order of change. And while the word *constant* appears in both statements, the meaning of the word is not the same. In one case, we are dealing with something constant in *existence,* physical or metaphysical; in the other case, with something constant in *function* and operation. One is a form of independent being; the other is a formula of description and calculation of inter-dependent changes.

Bibliography

Adler, Alfred. *Understanding Human Nature*, trans. W. Beran Wolfe (Greenwich, Conn.: Fawcett Publications, 1965).

Allen, Gina. "The Night I Saw the Light," *Free Inquiry* (Spring 1987).

Amiel, Henri Frederic. *Amiel's Journal*, trans. Mrs. Humphry Ward (New York: Macmillan, 1909).

Blackham, H. J. "A Definition of Humanism," in *The Humanist Alternative: Some Definitions of Humanism*, Paul Kurtz, ed. (Buffalo, N.Y.: Prometheus Books, 1973).

Blau, Joseph A. "Toward a Definition of Humanism," in Kurtz, *The Humanist Alternative*.

Bojer, Johann. *The Great Hunger* (1919).

Bronowski, Jacob. "The Fulfillment of Man," Conway Memorial Lecture, 1954.

Brooke, Rupert. *The Collected Poems of Rupert Brooke* (New York: Dodd, Mead, 1945).

Browning, Robert. "Saul," in *The Complete Works of Robert Browning*, vol. 4 (Athens, Ohio: Ohio University Press, 1973).

Camus, Albert. *The Rebel: An Essay on Man in Revolt*, trans. Anthony Bower (New York: Vintage Books, 1956).

Comte, Auguste. *The Positive Philosophy*, vol. 3, trans. Harriet Martineau (London: George Bell & Sons, 1896).

Cousins, Norman. "A Game of Cards," in *This I Believe*, Edward P. Morgan, ed. (New York: Simon and Schuster, 1952).

Darrow, Clarence. *The American Treasury, 1455-1955,* Clifton Fadiman, ed. (New York: Harper & Brothers, 1955).

———. *The Great Quotations,* George Seldes, ed. (New York: Pocket Books, 1967)

Darrow, Clarence, and Wallace Rice. *Infidels and Heretics: An Agnostic's Anthology* (Boston: Stratford Company, 1929).

Darwin, Charles. *The Descent of Man and Selection in Relation to Sex* (New York

Appleton, 1897).

de Ford, Miriam Allen. "Heretical Humanism," in Kurtz, *The Humanist Alternative*.

Dewey, John. *Reconstruction in Philosophy* (New York: Henry Holt, 1920).

———. *Experience and Nature* (Chicago: Open Court Publishing, 1925).

———. *A Common Faith* (New Haven: Yale University Press, 1934).

d'Holbach, Paul Henry Thiry. *Good Sense,* trans. H. D. Robinson (1772).

Diderot, Denis, *Rameau's Nephew,* trans. Jacques Barzun and Ralph H. Bowen (Indianapolis: Bobbs-Merrill, 1964).

Edison, Thomas A. Seldes, *The Great Quotations.*

Einstein, Albert. *Living Philosophies* (New York: Simon and Schuster, 1937).

Eliot, George. *A George Eliot Miscellany: A Supplement to Her Novels,* F. B. Pinion, ed. (Totowa, N.J.: Barnes & Noble, 1982).

Eliot, T. S. *Four Quartets* (London: Faber & Faber, 1944).

Ellis, Albert, "The Testament of a Humanist," *Free Inquiry* (Spring 1987).

Epicurus. *The Philosophy of Epicurus,* trans. George K. Strodach (Evanston, Il.: Northwestern University Press, 1963).

Ericson, Edward L. "Ethical Humanism," in Kurtz, *The Humanist Alternative.*

Flew, Antony. "Theology and Falsification," in *New Essays in Philosophical Theology,* Antony Flew and Alasdair Macintyre, eds. (New York: Macmillan, 1955).

Freud, Sigmund. *New Introductory Lectures on Psycho-analysis,* trans. W. J. H. Sprott (New York: W. W. Norton, 1933).

Fromm, Erich. *The Art of Loving* (New York: Harper & Brothers, 1956).

———. *The Revolution of Hope* (New York: Harper & Row, 1968).

Gordon, George, Lord Byron. *Poetical Works* (London: Oxford University Press, 1904).

Haydon, A. Eustace. *Biography of the Gods* (New York: Macmillan, 1945).

Henley, William Ernest. *Poems* (New York: Scribner's, 1898).

———. *In Memoriam Margaritae Sorori* (New York: Charles Scribner's Sons, 1920).

Hoffer, Eric. *The True Believer* (New York: Harper and Row, 1951).

———. *Between the Devil and the Dragon: The Best Essays and Aphorisms* (New York: Harper and Row, 1982).

Hook, Sidney. "On Defining Humanism," in Kurtz, *The Humanist Alternative.*

Huxley, Julian. *Religion Without Revelation* (London: Ernest Benn, 1927).

———. "The Faith of a Humanist," radio address, 1960.

Huxley, Thomas Henry. "Nineteenth Century," reprinted in *Science and the Christian Tradition* (New York: Appleton, 1896).

———. *Method and Results: Essays* (New York: Appleton, 1897).

———. *Evolution and Ethics and Other Essays* (New York: Appleton, 1916).

Ingersoll, Robert Green. *Works of Robert G. Ingersoll* (New York: AMS Press, Inc., reprint of the Dresden Edition, 1900–1911).

Khayyam, Omar. *The Rubaiyat,* 4th ed., trans. Edward Fitzgerald (London: B. Quaritch, 1879).

Kluckhohn, Clyde. *Mirror for Man* (New York: McGraw-Hill, 1949).

Kurtz, Paul. "Humanism and the Moral Revolution," in Kurtz, *The Humanist Alternative.*

———. *In Defense of Secular Humanism* (Buffalo, N.Y.: Prometheus Books, 1983).

————. "The Affirmations of Humanism," *Free Inquiry* (Spring 1987).

Lamont, Corliss. *Man Answers Death: An Anthology of Poetry* (New York: Philosophical Library, 1936).

————. "Naturalistic Humanism," *The Humanist* 31, no. 5 (Sept.–Oct. 1971).

Lippmann, Walter. *A Preface to Morals* (New York: Macmillan, 1929).

London, Joan. *Jack London and His Times* (Seattle: University of Washington Press, 1939).

Lucretius, *On the Nature of Things,* trans. Cyril Bailey (Oxford: Clarendon Press, 1910).

Masters, Edgar Lee. *Spoon River Anthology* (New York: Macmillan, 1915).

McGinley, Phillis. *Times Three* (New York: Viking, 1960).

Mencken, H. L. *Prejudices: Third Series* (New York: Knopf, 1922).

————. Fadiman, *The American Treasury.*

Mill, John Stuart. *On Liberty* (London: John W. Parker and Son, 1859, reprinted by Prometheus Books, Buffalo, N.Y., 1986).

————. *Utilitarianism* (London: Parker, Son, and Bourn, 1863, reprinted by Prometheus Books, Buffalo, N.Y., 1987).

Miller, Henry. *The Wisdom of the Heart* (New York: New Directions, 1941).

Murray, Gilbert. *Humanist Essays* (London: Allen & Unwin, 1964).

Protagoras. *Oxford Dictionary of Quotations,* 2nd ed. (Oxford: The Clarendon Press, 1955).

Reese, Curtis W. *Humanism* (Chicago: Open Court Publishing, 1926).

————. *Humanist Religion* (New York: Macmillan, 1931).

Russell, Bertrand. *The Conquest of Happiness* (New York: Horace Liveright, 1930).

————. "The Faith of a Rationalist," radio address, 1947.

————. *Why I Am Not a Christian and Other Essays on Religion and Related Subjects* (New York: Simon and Schuster, 1957).

————. *The Autobiography of Bertrand Russell* (London: Allen & Unwin, 1975).

Schopenhauer, Arthur. *Philosophy of Arthur Schopenhauer,* trans. Belfort Bax and Bailey Saunders (New York: Tudor Publishing Co., 1936).

Seneca. *Ad Lucilium Epistulae Morales,* trans. Richard M. Gummere (New York: G. P. Putnam's Sons, 1925).

Slaten, Arthur Wakefield. *Words of Aspiration* (New York: privately printed, 1927).

Sophocles. *The Tragedies of Sophocles,* trans. Richard C. Jebb (Cambridge: Cambridge University Press, 1904).

————. *The Three Theban Plays,* trans. Robert Fagles (New York: Viking Press).

Spencer, Herbert. *The Data of Ethics* (New York: Hurst and Company, 1879).

Thucydides. *The History of the Peloponnesian War,* trans. Richard Livingstone, ed. (London: Oxford University Press, 1943).

Twain, Mark. *The Mysterious Stranger* (Berkeley: University of California Press, 1982).

Weston, Robert. "Hymns for the Celebration of Life," responsive reading 421 (Boston: Beacon Press, 1954).

Wine, Sherwin. *Celebration* (Buffalo, N.Y.: Prometheus Books, 1988).

Index of Authors

223